WHAT THE
# ICEBERG
# HIDES

# WHAT THE
# ICEBERG
# HIDES

## THRIVING BEYOND THE SURFACE:
### Confidence, Career, and Community

**Dr. Inez González Perezchica**

RIOT OF ROSES
PUBLISHING HOUSE
SE3ATNGA
UNCEDED TONGVA TERRITORY
SOUTH WHITTIER, CALIFORNIA

Published by Riot of Roses Publishing House

What the Iceberg Hides - *Thriving Beyond the Surface: Confidence, Career, and Community*

Copyright © 2025, Dr. Inez González Perezchica


ISBN (paperback): *978-1-961717-38-1*
ISBN (ebook): *978-1-961717-39-8*

First Edition, 2025

To request permissions, you may contact the
Publisher at riotofrosesllc@gmail.com

For bookings or interviews, contact: gonzalez.inez@gmail.com

Printed in the United States of America

Edited by Brenda Vaca
Cover Design and Illustration by Eduardo Cumplido
Layout Design by Waseem Aziz at waseem@arrowupz.com

## DEDICATION

In memory of my ancestors—
my Mexican immigrant grandparents, *Manuel, Guadalupe, Hipólito,* and
*Florencia;* my great-grandmother, *Desideria;*
and my parents, *Juan* and *Teresa.*

Thank you for your sacrifices.
*Estoy aquí porque ustedes soñaron.* I am here because you dreamed.

And to my beloved sister, *Teresita,*
an educator whose love, wisdom, and example continue to guide me.

## Advanced Praise

So many have benefitted from Inez's wisdom over the years. We're elated she's put her insights in writing so even more people can gain from her practical and invaluable advice.

**Dr. Ted Martinez, Jr.**
**Lidia S. Martinez**
**Prominent Community Leaders**

As a recruiter, I've seen how much first-generation professionals can benefit from the kind of guidance Inez offers in this book. What the Iceberg Hides is a valuable guide for emerging professionals. The book captures the kind of honest, actionable advice that can change a person's career trajectory.

**Trevor Blair, CEO @ Blair Search Partners**

# Table of Contents

**Part One**

Self-Awareness &
Social Power —
Know Yourself

⌐_____
       **Page ... 1**

**Part Two**

Social Capital in
Action — Connect
and Contribute

⌐_____
       **Page...79**

**Part Three**

Your Story, Your
Future — Live with
Intention

⌐_____
       **Page...123**

## WHY I WROTE THIS BOOK

When you're the first in your family to go to college, you're often also the first to navigate professional spaces, negotiate a salary, ask for feedback, or understand that networking is a skill — not a personality trait. I didn't know these things early on, and I wish I had. So I'm writing the book I needed when I was figuring it out on my own.

As a leadership coach, educator, and mentor, I've had the privilege of working with people from all walks of life — college students just beginning their journeys, professionals navigating career pivots, and community leaders stepping into greater responsibility. Many came to me at a crossroads, in the midst of a transition, unsure of their next move.

Despite their talent, ambition, and drive, I noticed a recurring theme: they felt stuck.
Not from a lack of ability.
Not from a lack of desire.
But because they lacked access to the right people, the right networks, and often, the right perspective.

They didn't recognize their own brilliance. More importantly, they didn't know how to leverage it. That realization became the foundation of my work. Over the years, I've had hundreds of conversations—some as brief as twenty minutes—that made a real difference. I found myself sharing the same guidance again and again. Not as a secret formula, but as practical wisdom rooted in real life.

That's why I wrote this book.

I want more people  — especially first-generation college students, emerging professionals, and those from underrepresented communities — to have access to the insights, encouragement, and strategies that can help them thrive. I want this book to be a tool for anyone on a journey of growth, whether you're just starting out or finding your way forward.

This book is also for mentors, educators, supervisors, and coaches who want to support the next generation. We all have the power to open doors for others; the key is to be intentional about it.

If you've ever wondered what to say to a young person who's trying to find their way, I hope this book gives you a starting point. Sometimes, a single honest and encouraging conversation can shift a person's direction entirely.

And if you're the one feeling stuck, invisible, or unsure of your next step, know this: you're not alone — and you are more than enough. You may simply need new tools, new language, or a fresh perspective to help you move forward. This book is for you.

Together, we'll explore the power of social capital — what it is, why it matters, and how you can intentionally build a thriving, supportive community around you. When you invest in people, you invest in possibility. And when you learn to tap into the network that surrounds you, you begin to understand that you were never meant to do this alone.

This book is not a guide to schmoozing or selling yourself. It's an invitation to show up with courage, to listen deeply, to build trust, and to invest in your community while allowing it to invest in you. That's where belonging begins. That's where leadership takes root.

Let's uncover what's beneath the surface — together.

# HOW TO USE THIS BOOK

I chose the iceberg metaphor for this book after giving a speech about my own story. I knew people saw the surface — the four degrees, the nonprofit executive role, the community leadership. But I also knew they didn't know the whole story. There's so much more beneath it — the pain, rejection, and doubt that shaped the journey.

As a coach, I've learned that we all have hidden stories. What others see is only the tip of the iceberg.

This book is meant to be more than words on a page. *What the Iceberg Hides* is both a guide and a personal workbook. Throughout the chapters, you'll find prompts and exercises designed to help you pause, reflect, and make the ideas your own, because reflection is where true learning takes root.

Think of these moments as a gift you give yourself: a chance to slow down, listen to your thoughts, and connect the dots between your experiences and your aspirations. Reflection isn't always comfortable. It can stir up emotions you've pushed aside or moments you haven't fully processed. At times it may feel tender, even raw.

Be gentle with yourself in those moments. Listen to what your emotions are trying to tell you. Take breaks when needed. Return when you feel ready. Growth is rarely a straight line. It is a process of leaning in, stepping back, and then leaning in again. Over time, the words you write here will become more than notes or answers to prompts; they will become a map of your growth — a record of where you've been, what you've overcome, and where you're headed. One day, you may look back and be surprised by how far you've come, seeing in your own words the evidence of your resilience and evolution.

Reflection is one of the most powerful tools for growth. Without it, we risk moving through life on autopilot, never fully absorbing our lessons or recognizing the progress we've made. But when we pause, look inward, and name our experiences, we give meaning to our journey and direction to our future.

So take your time. Reflect deeply. Be honest with yourself. This workbook is not just about achieving success; it's about understanding yourself in ways that will help you define success on your own terms. It's about finding a path to happiness and fulfillment. That, to me, is true success.

Reflection is woven throughout the book, but so is structure. To give you a sense of where we're headed, the chapters are organized like a roadmap.

**Part I: Self-Awareness & Social Power — *Know Yourself***

Every journey begins beneath the surface. To thrive, you first need to understand yourself—your struggles, your values, and the resilience that has carried you this far. In this section, you'll uncover the hidden layers of your iceberg, reflect on the power you already hold, and see how relationships and social capital shape the opportunities ahead.

**Chapter 1: Beneath the Iceberg** — Explore the hidden layers of your story: the struggles, values, and lived experiences that make visible success possible.

**Chapter 2: Opportunity Flows Through People** — Recognize how doors often open through others and how investing in relationships creates opportunities beyond what's listed on a resume.

**Chapter 3: Social Capital — The Currency of Community —** Learn to see and nurture the invisible networks that quietly shape careers, access, and community power.

**Chapter 4: Leaving Your Comfort Zone, Discovering *You* —** Step into the unknown to reveal new layers of resilience, perspective, and connection that would otherwise remain hidden.

**Part II: Social Capital in Action — *Connect and Contribute***

Awareness alone isn't enough—you have to put it into motion. Success is not only about what you know or the degrees you earn; it's about how you transform knowledge, experiences, and connections into opportunities. This section explores how education, visibility, and reciprocity build momentum and help you open doors that credentials alone cannot.

**Chapter 5: What You Don't Know Can Hurt You —** First-generation college students and professionals often start without a roadmap. Success comes from mentors, sponsors, and social capital—not just degrees or job titles.

**Chapter 6: Learn to Brag (Without Feeling Like You're Bragging —** Reframe bragging as sharing your story with confidence so others see your value. Visibility matters.

**Chapter 7: Asking for Help Is a Strength, Not a Weakness —** Asking for help builds reciprocity and resilience. No one succeeds alone, and strong networks carry you further than effort alone.

**Part III: Your Story, Your Future** — *Live with Intention*

This final section brings everything together. It invites you to connect your experiences, values, and relationships to your evolving sense of purpose. Through reflection and guided exercises, you'll learn how to design your next chapter, navigate transitions with confidence, and align your future choices with what matters most.

**Chapter 8: What's Next?** — Whether you're finishing school, changing careers, or simply feeling stuck, this chapter shows how to focus on the next right step without needing a rigid five-year plan.

**Chapter 9: Finding Purpose** — Purpose isn't always a lightning bolt. More often, it's revealed in small choices, quiet moments, and consistent action. Learn how to recognize meaning in your journey and live with intention, even when the path ahead isn't perfectly clear.

# PART ONE

## SELF-AWARENESS & SOCIAL POWER — *KNOW YOURSELF*

*Ï am not afraid of storms for Ï am learning how to sail my ship.*
*Louisa May Alcott*

*Change begins with self-awareness. Before you can build meaningful connections, you need to understand yourself. Part Ï invites you to look beneath the surface—to uncover the experiences, values, and resilience that form your foundation. Take time to honor your achievements and your journey—the challenges and growth that have shaped who you are today. Here, you'll explore what lies beneath your iceberg, recognize how opportunity flows through people, and begin to see your own power more clearly.*

Chapter 1

# BENEATH THE ICEBERG

Success is often compared to an iceberg. Above the waterline, you see visible achievements: titles, awards, recognition. But below the surface lies the real story: the struggles, values, resilience, and relationships that make both success and fulfillment possible.

The surface shows only titles, achievements, and recognition, but that is just the tip of the iceberg. What lies beneath—relationships, resilience, values, and grit—is what truly sustains long-term fulfillment and meaningful success.

My own journey has shown me again and again that opportunity rarely comes from hard work alone. Of course, effort matters. But often the doors that opened for me did so because of people such as mentors, colleagues, and even acquaintances who created space for me to step through.

Fulfillment and success are rarely solo acts. Every achievement rests on the shoulders of mentors, peers, and opportunities created by others. When I earned recognition as a leader, what people noticed were the awards and the accolades. What they didn't see were the late nights, the mentors who guided me, the setbacks that tested me, and the networks that opened doors along the way. That is the iceberg of success: what is visible rests on a massive foundation of unseen effort and relationships.

The iceberg is a reminder not to measure success only by what is visible. Pay attention to what lies beneath: the investments, networks, and growth that make both success and fulfillment possible.

## My Iceberg

On the surface, here is what people see: I have four degrees, including one from Harvard. I have completed multiple leadership programs and held executive and community leadership roles across sectors. That is the visible part of my iceberg.

But beneath the surface is a very different story.

When I moved from México and started high school in the United States as a senior, everything changed. In Tijuana, I had been a leader in my school and my community. In San Diego, I felt invisible. My confidence evaporated. The negative stereotypes in the United States about Latinos chipped away at my sense of identity. I lost my voice, literally and figuratively.

As a freshman at the University of San Diego, I often spent the hours between classes in my car or in quiet, solitary spaces because I felt I didn't belong. On the outside, I smiled. Inside, I was shrinking.

It took years of personal development, stepping outside my comfort zone, and slowly rebuilding my confidence before I began to feel grounded in who I am. That journey, the one you cannot see at a glance, is what lies beneath my iceberg.

## What People Don't See

I have heard the comments:

"She's so lucky."

"He must have had connections."

"They just fell into that job."

"What a great pension—must be nice!"

People often dismiss achievements as nothing more than luck or privilege. And yes, sometimes privilege plays a role. But more often, what we see at the surface—the job title, the promotion, the comfortable retirement — is only the tip of the iceberg.

What we don't see is the courage it took to advocate for themselves in that performance review. Or the years they spent proving their own worth in spaces that didn't welcome them. Or the countless rejections before they heard a "yes."

Success might look like luck, but beneath the surface it is something far more complex: grit, persistence, adaptability, and moments of vulnerability that no resume will ever capture. Those unseen layers— shaped by struggle, resilience, and values—are what transform success into true fulfillment.

The iceberg is a reminder not to measure success only by what you can see. Pay attention to what is beneath: the unseen investments, the networks, and the growth that make it possible.

## Your Iceberg

You have an iceberg too. People may see your job title, your degrees, or your accolades and think they know your story. But do they know what it really took for you to get there?

Do you?

In my work with students, professionals, and leaders, I've found that many people haven't taken the time to reflect on what they have overcome. They skip past the hard parts. They rush to the next goal. And in doing so, they miss the chance to recognize the resilience and growth that already live inside them.

You deserve to reflect on your success, not to boast, but to own your story, to honor the road you have walked, and to understand the strength you carry.

So I will ask you again:

What is beneath your iceberg?
- Was it pushing through college while working two jobs?
- Navigating spaces where you were the only one who looked like you?
- Raising children while building a career?
- Recovering from rejection and coming back stronger?

All of that lives below the surface. And it matters.

## Reflection Matters

Looking beneath your iceberg is not just a feel-good exercise. It is a grounding practice, an act of self-awareness and a cornerstone of leadership.

When you take the time to acknowledge what you have overcome and achieved, three things happen:

- **You build confidence.** You stop waiting for others to validate you because you know, without question, what you have walked through.
- **You deepen compassion.** You start to see others with more curiosity and less judgment. You recognize that everyone carries something unseen.
- **You clarify your purpose.** When you remember what you have overcome, you see more clearly what matters most to you and why.

## You Are More Than They See

You have probably heard the phrase, "Don't judge a book by its cover." The same is true for people: don't judge an iceberg by its tip.

Whether you are at the start of your career, in the middle of it, or reflecting on decades of work, you have stories that have shaped you – some painful, some joyful, all valuable.

You may be someone who has never felt like you belonged. Someone who has doubted your worth in rooms that didn't reflect your identity or values. Someone who has achieved much but still feels there is more ahead.

I see you. And I want you to see yourself—not just through your resume, but through your resilience.

That is the first step to building real, lasting social capital: knowing your worth, owning your story, and recognizing that your journey has already made you someone others can trust, learn from, and connect with.

The world may only see the polished version of you. But you know what is beneath the surface. And now, it is time to honor that story.

## Moving Forward

If you look at what is beneath your iceberg, you will notice that many of those defining moments happened when you stepped outside your comfort zone, whether you meant to or not. Discomfort is often the birthplace of growth, and the very challenges you have faced have likely stretched you in ways you did not anticipate.

Your iceberg holds the truth of your story—the struggles, sacrifices, and strengths that made your visible accomplishments possible. By honoring what lies beneath, you gain clarity and compassion for your own journey, and you begin to see how those inner truths connect to the relationships that will shape your future. After all, opportunity often flows through people.

## REFLECTION & PRACTICE: DISCOVER YOUR ICEBERG

### Why This Matters

Your iceberg tells the truth about your journey: the victories people can see and the struggles, sacrifices, and growth they often cannot. By mapping your iceberg, you will honor the resilience that already lives inside you and see how your toughest moments have shaped your strength.

### Using This Space

Write directly here or in a separate journal if you need more room. Be honest and unfiltered—the story you capture here is for you alone.

Take your time; there's no single "right" way to do it.

## Step 1: Name Your Accomplishment

Choose one accomplishment you're proud of — a visible success such as earning a degree, a promotion, starting a business, raising a family, or buying your first home.

What do people see when they look at this success? Why is it meaningful to you?

## Step 2: Explore What Lies Beneath

Every success has unseen effort beneath it. Reflect on what made it possible. Write freely about:

What challenges or doubts did you face? What did you have to let go of or push through?

Who or what gave you strength to keep going?

Use the iceberg illustration to map your story — write your accomplishment above the waterline, and below it note the struggles, fears, and perseverance that fueled it.

**Here's a sample**

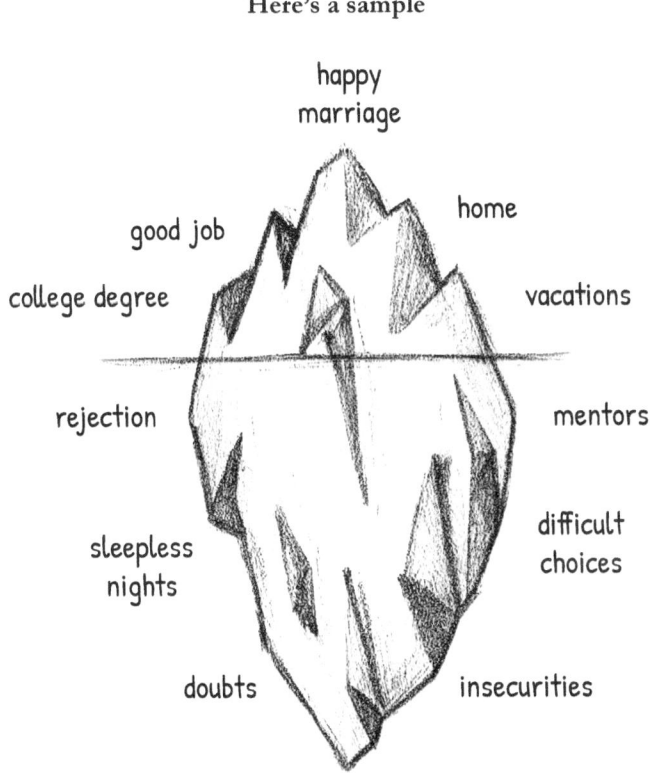

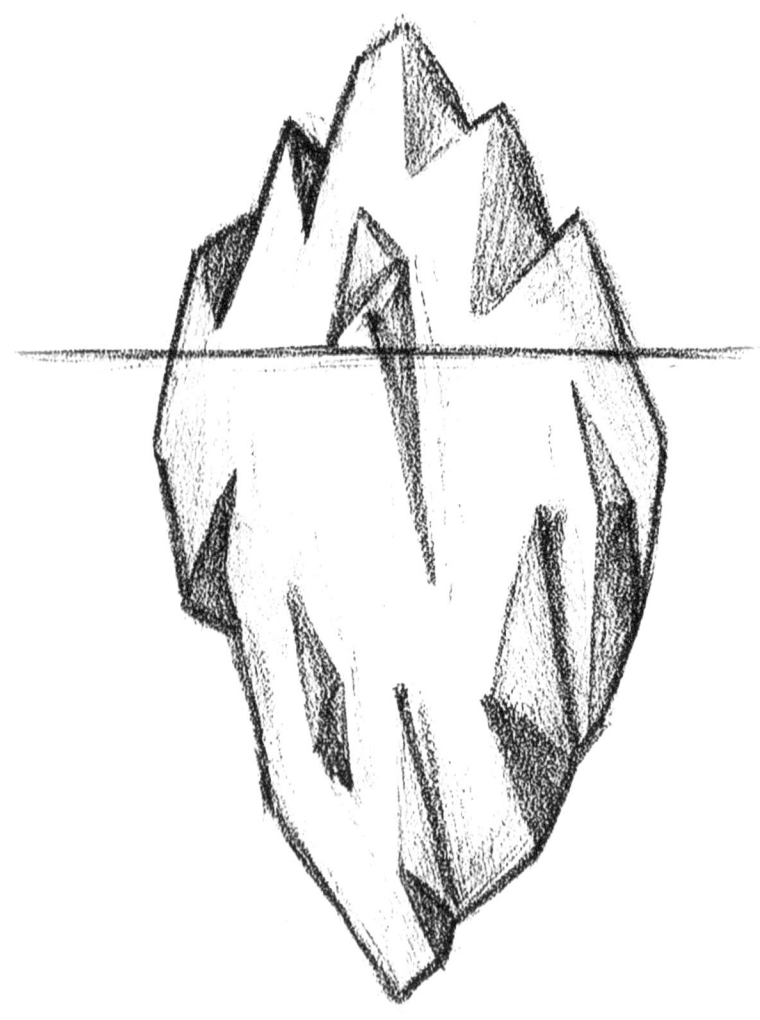

## Step 3: Reflect and Recognize Your Strength
Read back through what you've written.

After reflecting on what you've overcome, what feelings arise? What do they reveal about your strength? Is there a part of your story you've been minimizing or haven't given yourself credit for?

Write those insights down — these hidden truths matter.

# KEY TAKEAWAYS

Your iceberg holds both the visible wins and the hidden struggles that shape who you are.

Naming what lies beneath your values, habits, and experiences-builds self-awareness and confidence.

Reflection isn't a luxury. It's a practice that helps you see how far you've come and where you want to go.

# Notes & Reflections

Use this space to capture your thoughts, insights, or next steps

_____

_____

_____

_____

_____

_____

_____

_____

_____

_____

_____

_____

_____

_____

_____

_____

_____

_____

_____

_____

_____

Every reflection adds another layer beneath your iceberg.

# Chapter 2

# OPPORTUNITY FLOWS THROUGH PEOPLE

You may feel like you're walking your path alone at times, but many opportunities are shaped by others. Mentors who guide you, colleagues who recommend you, and friends who encourage you often play a role. Hard work opens some doors, but more often it's people who help you step through them.

When I was in college, I believed what many of us are taught: *Get your degree, and the career will follow.*

I thought that once I earned that piece of paper—the diploma—doors would swing open. Employers would line up with opportunities. That's the promise we're sold, right? Work hard, go to college, and the rest will take care of itself.

But when I graduated, reality hit hard. I had no idea how to actually start my career. I had only visited the career center on campus once, never practiced an elevator pitch, and never even thought about networking as a strategic tool. I assumed that if I checked all the academic boxes, the professional world would welcome me.

Luckily, life intervened in the form of a friend. Cristina knew I had just graduated and casually mentioned her employer was hiring. I hadn't asked her for help—she simply offered. I applied, she put in a good word, and just like that, I got the job.

The pivotal moment came when I looked around and saw another friend—just as smart, just as hardworking—struggling to land her first career-relevant job. She had done everything "right" too, yet the doors weren't opening for her the way they had for me. That's when it hit me: the difference wasn't ability — it was about access.

Hard work and degrees matter, but access through people often makes the difference between being overlooked and being considered. Cristina's referral didn't guarantee me the job, but it gave me a chance to be seen. That contrast opened my eyes: relationships can be the bridge between potential and recognized opportunity.

And here's the part that matters for you: if you've ever wondered why some people seem to "get ahead" faster, it's not necessarily because they're smarter or more talented. Often, it's because someone vouched for them, said their name in the right room, or opened a door they couldn't open alone. That insight changed how I approached my career. I stopped thinking of networking as an optional extra and started seeing it as part of the work itself. Relationships aren't just nice to have—they are bridges to opportunity, support, and growth.

Like an iceberg, so much of that opportunity lies beneath the surface. On the outside you see a job title or a success story, but underneath are the conversations, introductions, and acts of trust that make those visible wins possible.

## Becoming an Opportunity Connector

Seeing that contrast lit a fire in me. I didn't just want to benefit from other people's help; I wanted to create opportunities for myself and, eventually, for others. In the early days, help tended to find me. But I knew I couldn't rely on luck or generosity alone. I had to learn how to ask, how to follow through, and how to become the kind of person who opened doors for others, not just walk through them.

Years ago, I met Tatiana, a recent college graduate beginning her job search. She was talented, driven, and full of promise. And she wasn't afraid to ask for help. What she lacked wasn't potential or initiative—it was access.

I saw it immediately. So I made a few calls. I connected her with people I trusted, professionals who could offer guidance and openings in her field. To her credit, she followed up and followed through. She made the most of every introduction, even traveling to Washington D.C., where I lived at the time. Eventually, I introduced her to my boss, and a few weeks later she was hired.

Watching her career grow reminded me: opportunity often travels person to person, connection to connection.

## A Connector's Mindset

Don't just look for who can help you. Ask yourself: *Who can I open a door for?*

Earlier in my career, while working in the office of a U.S. Congressman, I began to think about what I call *opportunity positions*, roles that may look small on paper but can serve as powerful launchpads for someone's career.

I saw the receptionist position as one of those roles. Instead of hiring only candidates with political experience, I looked to the CalWORKs program, which connects low-income families to employment and support services. I hired a CalWORKs participant who brought reliability, warmth, and a hunger to learn. Yes, it took extra training, but it was absolutely worth it. I didn't just fill a position, I helped someone take a first step toward stability and growth.

Later, while leading a nonprofit, I hired Christine, who came from retail. She was friendly, curious, and proactive. She was promoted again and again, eventually becoming a director. She always had the potential. She just needed someone to give her a chance.

That's what happens when we invest in people. When we look beyond resumes and degrees and notice character, attitude, and potential.

One thoughtful decision can change the trajectory of someone's life. If you're in a position to hire, think about how you can be an opportunity connector.

## The Power of Weak Ties

Here's another piece of the puzzle: not all connections carry the same weight.

There's a classic idea in sociology called the strength of *weak ties*.[1] The insight is simple: your close friends usually know the same people you do. Weak ties—acquaintances, classmates, colleagues you met once—connect you to entirely different networks. Research shows people are more likely to land a job through a weak tie than a close friend. Not because friends don't want to help, but because they usually can't. They're swimming in the same pool. Weak ties are bridges.

---

[1] Sociologist Mark Granovetter first introduced the idea of "weak ties" in his 1973 article *The Strength of Weak Ties* in the *American Journal of Sociology*. He later expanded this work in his book *Getting a Job: A Study of Contacts and Careers* (1974, updated editions), showing how people often found jobs through acquaintances rather than close friends because weak ties connect us to new circles and opportunities.

Weak ties expand your reach. They connect you to people, places, and possibilities you'd never access through close friends alone.

Later, we'll go deeper into the concept of social capital. For now, think of it simply as the trust, goodwill, and access that flow through relationships.

And remember: this isn't only about what you can gain. Every one of us can create opportunities for someone else. You might share a job posting, recommend a colleague for a panel, or simply say someone's name in a room where decisions are made. Weak ties can change a career—yours or someone else's.

## A Strong Resume Will Help You Win Your Dream Job

A resume is more than a list of jobs—it's your professional passport. It tells the story of where you've been and hints at where you're headed. That's why it's worth the effort to make sure it reflects you well. A strong resume doesn't appear overnight; it's built over time, as you intentionally add skills, projects, and experiences that move you toward your goals.

In my early career, I realized that understanding budgets, supervising staff, and managing projects were essential if I wanted to keep advancing. Jobs that didn't offer me that experience, I didn't stay in for long.

The same is true for students I've mentored. Some want to be journalists, but their resumes show no writing or media experience at all. I tell them to start volunteering, contribute to campus media, or look for ways to gain relevant experience. Your resume should reflect not just your ambitions but the steps you're taking toward them.

That's why I encourage you to review your resume each year and ask yourself:

- Does it reflect where I'm headed, not just where I've been?
- If someone introduced me, would this back up their recommendation?

Employers often receive hundreds of resumes for a single role and many use software to scan for keywords like job titles, skills, and qualifications. So yes, your resume needs to stand out. But here's the truth: while a resume can establish you as a qualified candidate, it's often people—mentors, advocates, connectors—who move you from being a qualified candidate to being the one who gets the interview.

## Final Thoughts: You Are Not Alone

You don't have to figure out your next opportunity by yourself. Opportunities usually come through people.

But it's not about using people. It's about building relationships rooted in mutual respect and reciprocity. It's about showing up for others, so when your time comes, they show up for you.

If you're job searching, pivoting careers, or stepping into something new, remember this: you already know someone who knows someone. Your network is bigger than you think. Your next opportunity might be just one conversation away. So go ahead: make the list. Start reaching out. Plant the seeds. When you water relationships with time, trust, and authenticity, opportunity blooms.

## Final Reminder

Opportunities most often travel through people—friends, acquaintances, mentors, even weak ties. Behind each door that opens is a web of trust and connection. That invisible force has a name: *social capital.*

In the next chapter, we'll explore what social capital really means, why it matters, and how you can start building it with intention.

## REFLECTION & PRACTICE: OPPORTUNITY FLOWS THROUGH PEOPLE

### When Have Doors Opened for You?

Take a few minutes to write about the role of people in your opportunities.

Who first opened a door for you in your education or career, and how did their support shape your path?

Have you ever opened a door for someone else? What happened?

Looking back, how has community—not just credentials—helped you move forward?

## Build Your Opportunity Map

Map the people in your life who could help open doors—and the doors you could open for them.

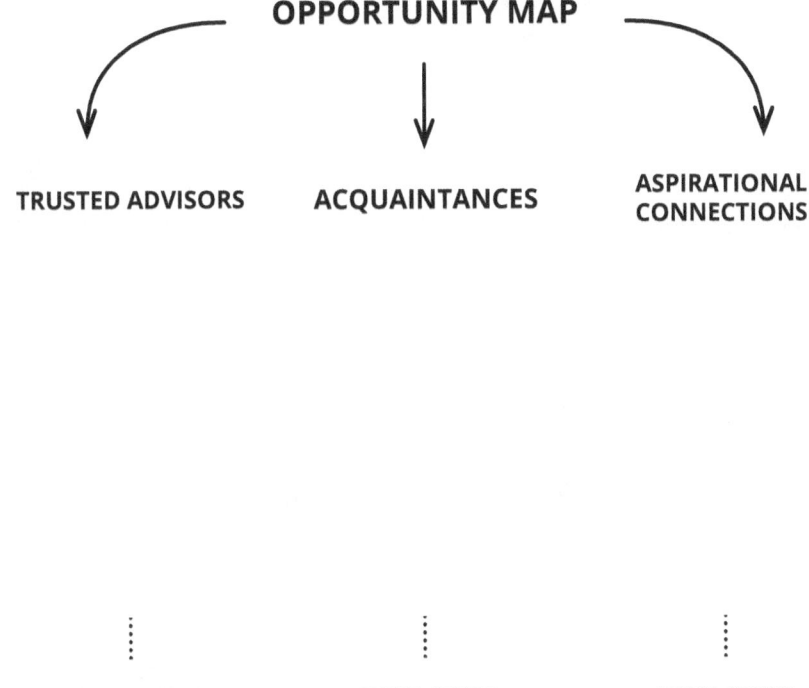

## Try It This Week: Map to Action

Choose one or two small steps this week to activate your network.

- Reconnect with someone you know (send an email, text, or invite them for a coffee chat).

- Expand your network—reach out to one weak tie. Write their name here:



- Open a door for someone else (recommend, encourage, connect).


Don't wait for the perfect moment. Begin now. Even one message or introduction can open a new door—for you or for someone else.

# KEY TAKEAWAYS

Opportunities often come through people. The connections you build can open doors that effort alone might not unlock.

Relationships are long-term assets. Mentors, sponsors, and peers can shape your path in ways you may not see right away.

Investing in others matters. The more you support, encourage, and connect people, the more likely opportunities will flow back to you in unexpected ways.

# Notes & Reflections

*Use this space to capture your thoughts, insights, or next steps*

_____

_____

_____

_____

_____

_____

_____

_____

_____

_____

_____

_____

_____

_____

_____

_____

_____

_____

_____

_____

*Every reflection adds another layer beneath your iceberg.*

# Chapter 3

# SOCIAL CAPITAL — THE CURRENCY OF COMMUNITY

I f opportunity flows through people, then social capital is the currency that carries it.

The term may sound academic, but its meaning is simple: the community you build is one of the most valuable forms of capital you will ever have. The relationships you nurture—whether deep bonds or small interactions—can open doors, offer guidance, and shape your life in ways you might never expect.

At its core, social capital is the value that comes from your relationships: the trust, support, and access that grow when you're part of a network— whether that's your school, workplace, neighborhood, or professional circle. It costs nothing to build, but it requires intention, and the benefits can be life-changing.

Social capital is part of the iceberg too—mostly invisible, yet powerful. Others may see the promotion, the opportunity, or the success, but what they don't see are the networks of trust and goodwill beneath the surface making those moments possible.

## My Experience with Social Capital

Of the nine jobs I've held in my career, eight came through people I knew—not always close friends, but acquaintances, colleagues, mentors, or what researchers call weak ties. These connections weren't about quick gains or transactions. They developed organically, built on trust, and often appeared in the most unexpected ways.

For example, someone recommended me to a local Congressman who was looking for a District Director. At that time, I had just been laid off. I contacted everyone in my email list, let them know I was looking for a job, and shared my resume. By then I had built a strong reputation as a hard-working, reliable, responsible, community member.

Typically, District Directors have years of political experience. I did not. But because a person the Congressman respected recommended me, I got the interview—and the job. That opportunity didn't come from a job board. It came through social capital.

## The Ripple Effect

The beauty of social capital lies in its ripple effect. When you invest time in building genuine relationships—listening, helping, and creating value without expecting immediate returns—you create a network that not only supports you but also amplifies your ability to support others.

That's where leadership begins: not with titles or authority, but with the willingness to connect, serve, and grow alongside others.

And yet, despite being hyper-connected through technology, many people feel profoundly isolated—from opportunities, from each other, and from the kinds of networks that foster upward mobility, confidence, and well-being. The fabric of community that once held us together is fraying in a world that often prioritizes individualism over collective care.

## Rethinking Networking

Some people recoil at the word "networking," dismissing it as fake or self-serving. And when it's done superficially, it can be. But authentic networking—the kind I've practiced and seen transform lives—is rooted in trust, reciprocity, and shared purpose.

It's not about collecting contacts. It's about cultivating relationships. It's about showing up for others, being generous with your time and knowledge, and creating space for mutual growth.

You don't need money, charisma, or privilege to build social capital. You need courage, intentionality, and a willingness to show up.

## What Social Capital Looks Like

Social capital might sound abstract, but you see it every day:

- **On campus:** A professor forwards an internship posting you didn't know about. A classmate shares a tip that helps you land a scholarship.
- **At work:** A colleague introduces you to a manager in another department. A senior leader nominates you to present because they know your work.
- **In community:** A neighbor connects you to a reliable mechanic. A parent at school tells you about an after-school program that helps with childcare.
- **In careers:** Instead of applying online and waiting, someone you know forwards your resume to the hiring manager — and you get an interview.

## What Is Social Capital?

Sociologist Pierre Bourdieu[2] described social capital as a resource often concentrated among elites, passed down like wealth, and difficult for working-class people to access. But lived experience—and newer research—show us something important: while social capital may not be evenly distributed, it can be built intentionally.

It's the professor who writes you a recommendation letter. The colleague who tips you off to a job opening. The neighbor who checks in when you're going through a rough time. Once you understand it, you begin to see your community differently—not just as a group you belong to, but as a network of relationships that can open doors and create opportunities.

Social capital isn't about who you know. It's about who knows you and trusts you enough to share valuable information or connections.

## Discovering Social Capital

In 2013, I joined Cal State Fullerton as an administrator. After years in public service, media, and nonprofit leadership, I finally felt I had found my purpose: working with first-generation college students.

It was there that I came to understand the transformative power of social capital. I had always known networking mattered, but now I had the language and research to support what I had lived. Social capital is a different kind of capital—often as valuable as money, sometimes more.

Yet so few people understand its power. It isn't taught in most

---

[2] Pierre Bourdieu's landmark book *Distinction: A Social Critique of the Judgement of Taste* (1979; English translation, 1984) explored how our tastes and lifestyles reflect deeper forms of cultural and social capital.

classrooms. It's not something first-gen college students usually hear about from parents or counselors. But it is essential.

When I began speaking to students about this concept, it resonated deeply. Many were juggling school, work, and family obligations. They rarely had time—or knew how—to build a network. But once they learned about social capital, they began to see themselves differently: not just as students, but as community builders in the making.

## Reciprocity in Action

One of the core principles of social capital is reciprocity—the rhythm of giving and receiving that sustains trust and connection. Relationships flourish when there's mutual exchange. Not immediate payback, but a long-term cycle of support.

At Cal State Fullerton, I watched reciprocity come alive. Students who landed competitive internships recommended classmates to take their place when they moved on. Alumni circled back to mentor the next generation. Over time, the Latino Communications Institute became powerful not just because of faculty or staff, but because of the culture of peer mentoring and resource-sharing that students created.

I carried this principle into my work with professionals. For decades, I've been part of MANA de San Diego (MANASD), an organization dedicated to Latina leadership. One of MANASD's cornerstones is reciprocity: participants in its leadership development program are asked to pay it forward. And they do—by returning as volunteers, serving on the Board of Directors, and mentoring college students. That cycle of support ensures the program's impact keeps multiplying long after the training ends.

The principle is the same whether you're a student or a seasoned professional: strong communities thrive when people invest in one another. In healthy networks, doors don't just open for you—they open because of you.

## The Shadow Side: Free Riding[3]

Reciprocity also has a shadow side: the free rider. Free riders benefit without contributing. They take advantage of generosity without giving back, and over time that erodes trust and weakens the very network that helped them.

This isn't about keeping score—it's about being intentional. Ask yourself:
- Am I giving as much as I'm receiving?
- Do I show gratitude when people support me?
- Am I helping others grow—or mostly focused on my own goals?

True social capital isn't transactional, but it is relational and reciprocal. It thrives when people are thoughtful, generous, and accountable.

## Building Social Capital in Practice

You can start building social capital today. You don't need a title or a big platform. You just need to take small, intentional steps.

---

[3] The economist Mancur Olson first described the "free rider problem" in his 1965 book *The Logic of Collective Action.* He explained how people can enjoy the benefits of a group or community without contributing to it, which makes sustaining collective goods more difficult. Decades later, political scientist Robert Putnam brought the idea into conversations about community life and democracy. In *Bowling Alone: The Collapse and Revival of American Community* (2000), he showed how declining participation in civic groups weakens social capital and increases the risk of free riding.

**For Students:**
- Introduce yourself to a professor.
- Join a student club or professional association.
- Go to a campus event and talk to one new person.
- Ask someone you admire for a coffee chat.
- Follow up when people give you advice.

**For Professionals:**
- Attend industry events.
- Be clear about what you're looking for.
- Keep your resume ready.
- Stay connected with peers who are also rising in their fields.

At your next event, set a small goal: meet two new people and ask each one thoughtful questions. Follow up within 48 hours. Small steps compound into big opportunities.

Networking may not always feel comfortable, but it gets easier with practice. Start with your peers—that often feels less intimidating than approaching an executive. But don't stop there. At your next conference, read the speaker list. Pick two people you want to meet. Show up early to their panel or stay after their presentation, introduce yourself to the speaker(s), ask a thoughtful question.

Belonging is built not only by you, but also by the places that make room for you.

## The Well-Being Connection

Relationships are not just helpful for your career—they are essential for your health and happiness.

In 2023, U.S. Surgeon General Dr. Vivek Murthy[4] declared loneliness and social isolation a public health crisis. He warned that the lack of connection is as dangerous as smoking fifteen cigarettes a day. Loneliness increases the risk of heart disease, stroke, dementia, depression, and early death.

Decades of research, including the famous Harvard Study of Adult Development[5], show that strong relationships are the most consistent predictor of happiness and well-being.

You can be rich in social capital—even if your bank account says otherwise.

By now, you've seen how opportunity flows through people and why social capital is such a powerful force in shaping our lives. Success isn't just about what you know—it's about who walks alongside you, who opens doors, and how you show up for others in return.

But relationships are only part of the story. The other part is you—your willingness to step into new spaces and meet new people. In the next chapter, we'll explore what happens when you leave the comfort of the familiar and step into the unknown—not just to grow your network, but to grow yourself.

---

[4] In 2023, U.S. Surgeon General Dr. Vivek Murthy issued an advisory declaring loneliness and social isolation a public health crisis. (U.S. Department of Health and Human Services, Our Epidemic of Loneliness and Isolation: The U.S. Surgeon General's Advisory on the Healing Effects of Social Connection and Community, 2023).

[5] The Harvard Study of Adult Development, which has followed participants for more than 80 years, found that the strongest predictor of happiness and health in life is the quality of our relationships. See Robert Waldinger and Marc Schulz, The Good Life: Lessons from the World's Longest Scientific Study of Happiness (Simon & Schuster, 2023).

## REFLECTION & PRACTICE: BUILDING YOUR SOCIAL CAPITAL

### Reflection 1: Your Support Circle

This is your personal journal space. Write directly in this book or in a notebook—what matters is capturing your thoughts honestly. Don't just think through the questions, write them down. Putting ideas on paper makes them real and easier to act on.

Who are the five people you turn to for support, advice, or encouragement?

♥ _____

♥ _____

♥ _____

♥ _____

♥ _____

What makes those relationships strong?

When was the last time you helped someone without expecting anything in return?

Think about a time someone helped you. How did that support shape your journey?

What professional or academic opportunities have come your way through someone you know?

## Reflection

Are you nurturing your connections regularly - or only reaching out when you need help?

- ☐ I make time regularly.
- ☐ Only when I need something.
- ☐ Somewhere in between.

## Reflection 2: Generosity & Reciprocity

How have you paid it forward — extending support to someone new, even if they hadn't helped you first?

What small action can you take this week to strengthen or rekindle a relationship?

Take a moment to reflect on your reciprocity practice. How are you doing with the giving and receiving?

Reflect on how you give and how you receive. What do you want to continue, and what do you want to change?

## Reflection 3: Growth & Courage

What communities or networks bring value to your life? How do you show up for your community—and how could you show up more intentionally?

Who is one person you admire professionally that you could reach out to for an informational chat?

What fears or doubts come up when you think about networking or putting yourself out there?

## Try It This Week: Grow Your Social Capital

Commit to one or two specific actions.

**Step 1: Strengthen an existing relationship.** Who will I reach out to this week? How will I reconnect?

**Step 2: Create a new connection.** Who is someone I'd like to get to know better? What small step will I take?

**Step 3: Give back through reciprocity.** What is one way I can offer help, encouragement, or information?

# KEY TAKEAWAYS

Social capital is created through relationships—close ties, mentors, peers, and new connections.

Opportunities often flow through unexpected connections; even weak ties can open meaningful doors.

Building social capital takes intention: show up, give back, and nurture your network over time.

# Notes & Reflections

Use this space to capture your thoughts, insights, or next steps

_____

_____

_____

_____

_____

_____

_____

_____

_____

_____

_____

_____

_____

_____

_____

_____

_____

_____

_____

Every reflection adds another layer beneath your iceberg.

Chapter 4

# LEAVING YOUR COMFORT ZONE, DISCOVERING *YOU*

Growth begins where your comfort zone ends.

That's not just a catchy phrase—it's a truth I've seen again and again in my own life and in the lives of the people I've coached and mentored. Whether it's launching a business, going back to school, speaking up in a room full of executives, or leaving a relationship that no longer fits, true growth almost always comes with discomfort.

That moment when your heart races, your voice shakes, or you start to second-guess yourself. That's the stretch. It's your body and spirit stepping into unfamiliar territory. And while it rarely feels easy, it's often the first sign of transformation.

Fear doesn't always mean stop; sometimes it's a signal to move forward.

## Discomfort as a Signpost
We're quick to treat discomfort as danger. But not all discomfort is bad. Sometimes it's your soul asking for more: more challenge, more purpose, more alignment. The tension you feel might not be something to avoid—it might be something to walk toward.

Comfort has its place. There are seasons when stability is exactly what we need: caring for a loved one, raising children, healing from loss. But comfort should be a season, not a lifestyle. Many people stay in jobs, routines, or situations that feel familiar but no longer help them grow. The cost is high: missed opportunities, lost potential, and dreams left on hold.

Ask yourself often:
- Am I still learning?
- Am I still growing?
- Am I still happy?

If the answer is no, it might be time to stretch. You don't have to leap. Even a single small step outside your comfort zone rewires your confidence.

## My First Big Stretch

Some of the best decisions I've ever made began with a pit in my stomach.

Early in my career, I had what most would consider a dream job: a government role with good pay, a window office, and a supportive boss. But after a while, I realized I was no longer learning. I was young, yet already feeling the grip of golden handcuffs.

Still, I stayed. For nine years.

It wasn't until I experienced a personal loss that I found the clarity—and courage—to move. I left that stable role for a position at a Fortune 500 company. The pay was lower and the industry unfamiliar. It wasn't the right fit, and I resigned on my one-year anniversary without another job lined up.

Moving outside your comfort zone doesn't always look like a perfect next step. Sometimes it feels like a sideways move, or even a detour. But detours can teach you just as much as straight paths—and sometimes they take you exactly where you need to go.

That job was a detour—and you know what? Detours are okay. Stepping out of my comfort zone didn't always lead me directly where I thought I was going, but it moved me forward. Thanks to a friend's recommendation, I was hired as a marketing manager in an organization led by his father. Yes, you could call that nepotism—but it was also social capital at work.

My friend wouldn't have put his name on the line if he didn't believe I could deliver. Relationships may open doors, but skills, integrity, and a strong track record are what keep those doors open once you walk through. That opportunity became a turning point, setting me on a more fulfilling path—one I never would have found if I had stayed in the familiar instead of taking a chance on something new.

That experience reminded me that growth rarely happens in a straight line. The unexpected roles, the "off-track" jobs, the chances we almost overlook—those are often the very moments that stretch us, build confidence, and prepare us for what comes next.

That move taught me two lessons.

First, detours are still part of the path. Even when something doesn't work out the way you expect, you gain skills, resilience, and perspective.

Second, social capital pays off. A friend recommended me for a marketing role in his father's organization, and that opportunity set me on a more fulfilling path—one I never would have found if I hadn't stepped away from comfort.

Growth doesn't guarantee a straight line, but it does guarantee movement.

## The Risk of Staying Too Comfortable

Growth isn't about constantly chasing promotions or job changes. It's about evolving. It's about making sure your environment stretches you instead of numbs you.

I'll never forget a news story about the closing of FEDCO, a California-based membership department store. Dozens of employees—many of whom had been there 20 or 30 years—walked out in tears. I remember thinking: companies are not forever. The best investment you can make is in staying versatile, employable, and growing.

Your skills. Your relationships. Your reputation. Your ability to adapt. That's your true security.

## Leaving Home, Finding Myself

In my forties, I made a move that would change the course of my life. Not everyone can pack up and go—my circumstances made it easier because I was single and without children. For others, leaving home may require more planning or look very different. Growth doesn't always mean relocating; sometimes it's about finding other ways to stretch within your reality.

For me, that stretch came in the form of moving. I packed up a U-Haul and drove north to Los Angeles—just two hours away, but it felt like another world. I remember crying behind the wheel, heart heavy as I left behind everything familiar: my family, my friends, my routines. I told myself, "It's only for a year. Then I can come home."

But that one-year plan stretched into something much bigger.

That job in Los Angeles opened doors I never expected. It led me to Washington, D.C., where I walked the halls of Congress, worked on national policy, built deep relationships, and learned in ways I could never have imagined. I met changemakers, mentors, and lifelong friends. And perhaps most importantly—I grew.

Thirteen years would pass before I returned home to San Diego. By the time I came back, I had earned a master's degree from Harvard, a doctorate from Cal State Fullerton, and leadership experience in academia, nonprofit leadership, and national advocacy. None of that would have happened if I hadn't taken the risk to leave.

## Leaving Doesn't Mean Leaving Forever

One of the most powerful things I've learned is that moving away from home doesn't have to be permanent. You can go for a year, or two, or five—and then return with new skills, new experiences, and a stronger resume.

When you move away, you're not just changing your zip code. You're changing your perspective. You're stepping outside the norms and expectations that shaped you. You're learning who you are—without the familiar voices around you telling you who you've always been.

Our environment molds us. The people we see, the conversations we hear, the boundaries we accept—they all become part of our internal script. And while that can be beautiful, it can also be limiting. Sometimes, in order to hear your own voice clearly, you need to step away from the noise.

That's why I encourage people—especially young professionals and students—to leave their environment if they can. Not because home isn't good. But because leaving home, even temporarily, helps you discover who you are when no one is watching. It grows your social capital, expands your networks, and introduces you to mentors and allies you wouldn't have met otherwise.

## Is It Time?

Only you can answer these questions, but they're worth asking:
- Is it time to go back to school?
- Is it time to ask for that raise you've earned?
- Is it time to leave a job that no longer inspires you?
- Is it time to start the business, write the book, or launch the project you've been dreaming about?

These choices aren't easy. But neither is staying stuck. Small steps count just as much as big leaps.

## Growth Comes With Discomfort

Here's the truth: my best experiences weren't the easiest decisions to make.

Leaving San Diego wasn't easy. Moving to the East Coast wasn't easy. Driving that U-Haul to L.A. with tears in my eyes wasn't easy.

But they were worth it. Each of those moves challenged me in new ways. I had to rebuild my community, find my voice in new spaces, and navigate unfamiliar systems. But through those challenges, I found clarity, confidence, and purpose.

And that's why I say: some of the best decisions of your life will begin in discomfort.

## Your Comfort Zone Isn't Fixed

The good news? What feels uncomfortable now won't always be.

- The first time you speak up in a meeting, it's scary. The tenth time, it's empowering.
- The first time you introduce yourself to a stranger at a networking event, it's nerve-wracking. The twentieth time, it's natural.

Each stretch expands what's possible. Courage grows stronger with practice.

Start small. At a conference, introduce yourself to one speaker. At a social event, talk to someone outside your circle. Considering a new role? Do an informational interview. You don't have to be fearless—you just have to be willing.

Confidence doesn't come first. Action does. Courage grows stronger the more you practice it.

## Practical Tools for Navigating Fear & Doubt

- Reframe discomfort as a signal of growth. Ask, "What is this fear telling me?"
- Start small, stretch often. Break big leaps into small, repeatable actions.
- Borrow courage from others. Call a trusted friend or mentor before a big step. Accountability fuels action.

- Focus on the lesson, not the outcome. Success is in the learning. Even detours build skills and resilience.
- Track your wins. Keep a list of times you stretched. Review it whenever self-doubt creeps in.

## Reflection: What's Holding You Back?

Is there a place you've always wanted to live or work—but fear is holding you back?

You don't have to move across the country to grow—but you do have to move toward your growth. Even if it's just a short detour. Even if it's just for a season. That leap may lead you to exactly where you're meant to be.

Coming home after years away was powerful. I returned to the same city, but I was not the same woman. Each move had stretched me, reshaped me, and opened doors I never could have imagined. Leaving comfort didn't just grow my skills—it grew my networks, my perspective, and my sense of purpose.

And that's the point: the bigger the stretch, the more people, ideas, and opportunities you encounter. Growth rarely happens alone. In the next chapter, we'll explore how stepping out of comfort and into new spaces connects directly to the people who can help change your future.

## Final Thoughts

Growth doesn't live in the familiar. It lives at the edge of discomfort, where fear and possibility collide. Every time you stretch, you expand your capacity for what comes next.

But growth is only part of the story. The next step is learning how to turn that growth into opportunity. In the following chapter, we'll explore why a degree or job title alone isn't enough — and how mentors, sponsors, and social capital shape the doors that truly open for you.

## REFLECTION & PRACTICE: STRETCHING INTO GROWTH

### When Have You Stretched Yourself?
Think of a time you moved through fear into growth.
- What did you feel in the moment?
- What doubts or fears came up, and how did you move through them?
- What did you learn from that experience?
- How did it change you?

Don't just think about it—write it down. Naming your experience helps you learn from it.

## Climb Your Ladder

Growth happens one step at a time. Write next to the ladder action steps.

- **Start at the Bottom (Comfort):** This may be where you are now—your safe and familiar zone.
  *Example: Attending team meetings.*
- **Aim for the Top (Stretch):** This represents your goal—stepping into new territory.
  *Example: Presenting to senior leaders.*
- **Fill in the Middle Rungs:** Write down small, realistic actions that help you move upward.
  *Examples: Asking a question in a meeting; sharing an idea with colleagues; leading a small project.*
- **Climb Slowly:** Remember, you don't have to jump from comfort straight to stretch. Each action builds confidence and momentum for the next.

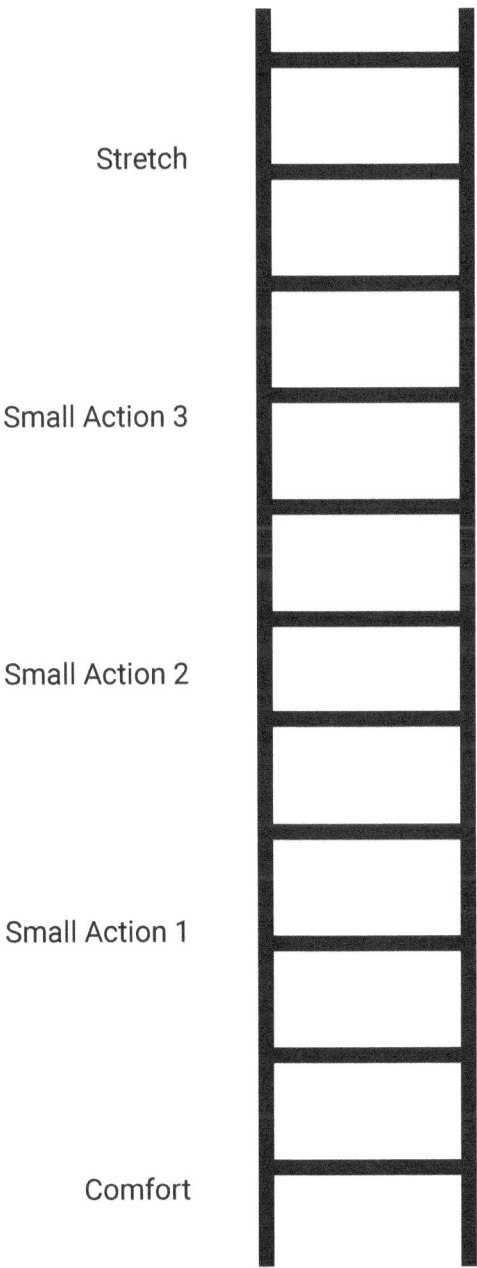

Stretch

Small Action 3

Small Action 2

Small Action 1

Comfort

**Reflection:** Which step feels easiest to take first? Which step feels most challenging—but also most exciting?

## Visioning Growth Beyond the Familiar

Reflect on how your environment shapes you. What might happen if you stepped into a new one?

- What change in environment or routine would stretch you?
- What might you gain personally or professionally?
- Who could support you in this change?
- Write a short vision statement describing what your life could look like after one year of choosing growth.

## Try It This Week: A Small Step Through Fear

Growth comes from action, not theory.

- **Identify your edge:** What's one thing you've been avoiding because it feels uncomfortable?
- **Choose your step:** What small action will you take this week?
- **Plan your support:** Who can you tell or who can help you stay accountable?

*Remember: the step doesn't need to be dramatic. Even small actions build momentum.*

## KEY TAKEAWAYS

Growth often begins with discomfort — fear and uncertainty can be signs you're moving toward transformation.

Comfort has its place, but staying too comfortable for too long can stall learning, limit opportunities, and hold back potential.

Stretching — whether through a move, a new role, or even small daily actions — expands your confidence, your networks, and your sense of what's possible.

# Notes & Reflections

Use this space to capture your thoughts, insights, or next steps

_____

_____

_____

_____

_____

_____

_____

_____

_____

_____

_____

_____

_____

_____

_____

_____

_____

_____

Every reflection adds another layer beneath your iceberg.

# PART TWO

## SOCIAL CAPITAL IN ACTION —
### *CONNECT AND CONTRIBUTE*

*We are what we repeatedly do. Excellence, then, is not an act but a habit.*
*Aristotle*

*In Part I, you looked inward. Now it's time to look outward—toward the systems, institutions, and networks that shape success. Degrees and credentials may open doors, but what you do once you step through matters more. This is where knowledge becomes opportunity, where contributions become visible, and where relationships turn into power. Awareness is only the first step. In this part, you'll see how to put that awareness into action—by building social capital with intention, seizing opportunities, and creating momentum that carries you forward.*

# Chapter 5

# WHAT YOU DON'T KNOW CAN HURT YOU

I'm embarrassed to admit that I didn't learn about negotiating a salary until my forties, when I took a Harvard class in negotiation. I know how that might sound—but it's my truth. As a first-generation college graduate and first-generation professional, no one had ever talked to me about negotiating pay.

Before that class, my attitude was simple: be grateful for the offer and accept the first number you're given. That's how I approached every job.

Now I know better, and I tell anyone who will listen: negotiating your salary is expected. Employers anticipate that a savvy applicant will negotiate. Even if the answer is no, the very act of asking signals that you know your worth and that you'll expect raises in the future.

That class was eye-opening. It showed me something I wish I had learned decades earlier: there are lessons and opportunities that talent and hard work alone won't unlock. You need information, guidance, and relationships to fill the gaps.

## The First-Gen Information Gap

First-generation college students often become first-generation professionals. That means they start out missing key information their parents couldn't provide, simply because they hadn't walked that road themselves.

This isn't a deficit of talent or motivation—it's an information gap. The rules of the game, from how to negotiate a salary to how to ask for a mentor, aren't always obvious. Recognizing that gap is critical—not as a limitation, but as a call to seek out what's missing.

That's where mentors and sponsors come in.

## Why Mentors (and Sponsors) Matter

Being the first in your family to attend college is not easy. Parents want to support, but often can't coach their children through applications, internships, or career decisions. The same is true in the workplace - your manager may not always be your best guide. Sometimes it's a colleague, an alum from your school, or a community leader who steps into that role.

- **Mentors** offer guidance, encouragement, and perspective.
- **Sponsors** go further — they use their influence to advocate for you, nominate you for opportunities, and speak your name in rooms you haven't yet entered.

Both are essential.

I've had both. Jack, one of my first supervisors, taught me the power of clear communication and gave me visibility with our Board of Directors. Lidia, a corporate executive, invited me to events and recommended me for a role in Los Angeles that changed my career trajectory.

Mentors and sponsors often see your brilliance before you can accept it yourself.

One of my former students, Franky, was serving in the Peace Corps when he asked me about grad school. I said, "Why not Harvard?" He hadn't even considered it. With encouragement, he applied — and he got in.

I knew he was a strong candidate, but I also knew he wouldn't have applied to that Ivy League school without someone encouraging him to stretch. That's what mentors do: they help you see more for yourself than you might have imagined.

The same is true in the workplace. I've seen professionals doubt whether they were "ready" for leadership until someone else insists they were. That belief, voiced by another, can shift how you see yourself.

## How to Find Mentors and Sponsors

Mentorship doesn't always begin with a formal ask. You don't need to say, *"Will you be my mentor?"* to start the relationship. What matters is connection, curiosity, and follow-through.

- **Start small:** Ask someone you admire for a short conversation about their career path. Follow up with thanks.
- **Look around you:** Professors, supervisors, alumni, community leaders, even peers can be mentors. Sponsors are often senior leaders, but they often grow out of relationships you already have.
- **Show promise:** Be reliable, proactive, and consistent. Mentors and sponsors invest in people who invest in themselves.

- **Be open to multiple guides:** You may have different mentors for different needs, and one sponsor who champions you at work.
- **Work intentionally with sponsors:** Share your goals. Ask what skills or experiences you should pursue. This gives them a roadmap for how to advocate for you.

The key is initiative. Mentors and sponsors rarely fall into your lap – you cultivate them by reaching out, building trust, and staying curious. Seek out both. And when the time comes, be both for others.

## Your Degree (or Job Title) Alone Is Not Enough

A degree can open the door, but it's rarely enough on its own. Likewise, landing the job is only the beginning. Building a career requires more than a title. In both college and the workplace, you must also build social capital — the relationships that help you learn, grow, and access opportunities.

Advice I often share with students and professionals alike:

### Don't overload yourself with jobs that just pay the bills.
- *Students:* Working more than 20 hours a week often limits your ability to network or take on leadership opportunities.
- *Professionals:* Getting buried in "busy work" can stall your growth and visibility.

### Be strategic about investments.
- *Students:* Sometimes a modest student loan frees up time to pursue internships or leadership roles.
- *Professionals:* A certification or course may stretch you now and open doors later.

## Use available resources.
- *Students:* Career centers, writing labs, student orgs.
- *Professionals:* Development programs, employee resource groups, and networking events.

Philosopher William James[6] believed that willpower gives us the ability to chart our lives—to be captains of our fate. He also emphasized habits as the building blocks of who we become. The routines you establish—showing up prepared, seeking mentors, staying curious—don't just shape experiences, they shape you.

When you realize that you can will yourself into growth, confidence, leadership, and new habits, you begin to take ownership of your path.


## The Catch-22 of Career Experience

I remember speaking with a student at Cal State Fullerton who worked at a furniture store and earned a good salary there. She was talented and motivated, but her 20+ hours a week left her little time for anything else. She wasn't in clubs, networking, or exploring leadership opportunities. As a senior, I could see immediately that she was missing career-relevant experience that would make her more competitive after graduation.

I encouraged her to use her last year in college differently: build social capital, get involved with campus organizations, and seek out a career-relevant internship. I also suggested she consider taking a modest student loan to reduce her work hours.

---

[6] Philosopher William James wrote about the power of the will and the role of habits in shaping our lives. In *The Principles of Psychology* (1890), he argued that our choices and repeated actions become the patterns that define who we are — what he called "a mass of habits."

Months later, she stopped me in the hallway. *"You may not remember me,"* she said, *"but you told me to take a loan. I did, and I quit my job. Now I'm more active on campus, and it's changing my experience. Thank you."*

Her story reminded me of the broader challenge many first-gen students face: the cycle of needing income while missing opportunities for growth.

Here's the cycle:
- Students need money → they work service or retail jobs.
- Professionals need stability → they stay in roles that pay but don't help them grow.

Meanwhile, peers with family financial support or stronger networks can afford to take unpaid internships or stretch roles that fast-track their growth.

Until systems change, you may need to get creative:
- Look for roles tied to your field, even part-time.
- Explore micro-internships, short-term projects, or stretch assignments.
- Volunteer strategically—even a few hours a week can build relevant experience.
- Reframe any job by highlighting transferable skills like teamwork, problem-solving, and leadership.

## Education Happens Outside the Classroom

If you're the first in your family to attend college, you may think clubs, lectures, or volunteering are "extra." They're not. These experiences build confidence, skills, and relationships.

The same is true in the workplace: volunteering for a project, attending a conference, or joining a professional association can build your reputation and expand your network.

## Good Debt vs. Lost Opportunity

Many students avoid loans at all costs. But excessive work hours can carry their own hidden price: missed opportunities. Sometimes a modest student loan is the smarter investment because it frees you to engage in internships and leadership roles.

The same applies to professionals. Spending money on a conference, course, or certification may feel risky, but if it positions you for growth, it's worth considering. This isn't about reckless spending—it's about intentional investment.

## Final Advice: Becoming

College and career aren't just about passing classes or collecting paychecks. They're about becoming → *more confident* → *more connected* → *more ready for what's next.*

When you graduate, or when you move up at work, it won't just be your degree or title that matters. It will be your social capital— the people who know your name, value your work, and believe in your future.

And you deserve that kind of support.

Some people question whether college is "worth it." The truth is more complex than the headlines. Degrees alone don't guarantee success, but research shows education often leads to greater earnings and mobility—especially when paired with social capital. (See Appendix A for more on the numbers and the debate.)

Knowledge, relationships, and investments may open doors—but being visible and known often determines how far you get once you step through.

Mentors and sponsors can speak your name in rooms you haven't entered, but you also need to learn how to speak for yourself. That means making your contributions visible.

In the next chapter, we'll explore how to reframe bragging—not as arrogance, but as authentic visibility—so that others can see and celebrate your impact.

## REFLECTION & PRACTICE: PREPARING FOR A SPONSOR CONVERSATION

Growth isn't just about what you achieve — it's about what you notice, how you act, and who you bring along. Use these prompts to pause, reflect, and map your next steps. Write out your answers. Clarity builds confidence — and preparation makes the conversation real.

Imagine you've been invited to meet with a sponsor tomorrow. How would you clearly and confidently describe your career goals?

What role do you hope to step into next? What skills, experiences, or training will help you get there?

How could a sponsor help you gain visibility or opportunities along the way?

## Your Education Investment

Reflect on your own (or your family's) educational and professional journey.

How has education or training shaped your opportunities so far?

Write your thoughts as an education return on investment (ROI) journal — not just about money, but about meaning, growth, and opportunity.

For example, you might reflect on how a class, mentor, or internship helped shape your confidence or opened a new path.

If you're considering further education or development, what do you hope it will give you — knowledge, connections, credentials, or something else?

What risks or sacrifices are involved, and what's the potential return?

## Reflection & Practice: Your Success Action Map

Choose at least one action you can commit to in the next month.

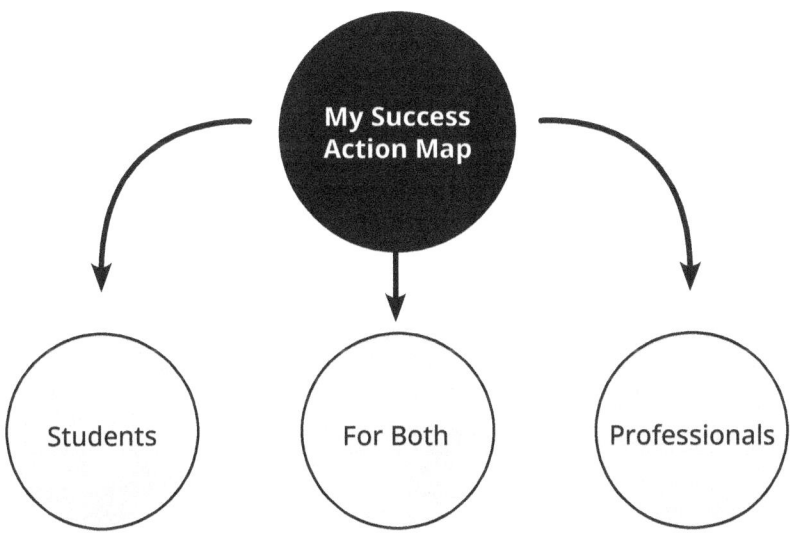

**Students**
- Attend a guest speaker event and introduce yourself afterward.
- Visit the career center for internship or job prep.
- Apply for at least one internship, fellowship, or job shadow.

**For Both**
- Identify 3 potential mentors or sponsors. Write down why each person stands out and one step you can take to connect.
- Schedule a conversation with a mentor or sponsor to share your goals. Be specific about the training or experiences you're seeking.
- Reflect on your long-term goals. What field do you want to explore? What experience do you need to get there?

**Professionals**
- Volunteer for a leadership role (even a small one) in a project or organization.
- Follow up with one professional contact you've recently met.
- Join or participate in a professional association this quarter.

# KEY TAKEAWAYS

Education opens doors, but growth deepens when paired with habits, relationships, mentors, and sponsors.

Mentors provide guidance and perspective; sponsors use their influence to advocate and create opportunities.

Strategic choices — investing in learning, seeking career-relevant experience, and making thoughtful financial decisions — expand your options for the future.

# Notes & Reflections

Use this space to capture your thoughts, insights, or next steps

_____

_____

_____

_____

_____

_____

_____

_____

_____

_____

_____

_____

_____

_____

_____

_____

_____

_____

_____

Every reflection adds another layer beneath your iceberg.

# Chapter 6

# LEARN TO BRAG (WITHOUT FEELING LIKE YOU'RE BRAGGING)

Y es, I called this chapter 'Learn to Brag' — and I know that word might make you uncomfortable. But that's the point. What feels like bragging is often just letting others see your hard work.

We've talked about how opportunity flows through people, and how social capital can change your trajectory. But social capital only works if others actually see your contributions. If you stay invisible, your network can't advocate for you. That's why it's time to tackle a skill most of us struggle with: learning to brag, strategically and authentically.

As a Latina, I was raised to be humble, respectful, and quiet. We were taught not to boast, not to draw attention to ourselves. We let our work speak for itself.

But here's the truth: work doesn't always speak for itself.

At different points in my career, I found myself as the "right hand" to powerful men—visionary leaders with big ideas. I was the #2 person, the one executing plans, managing follow-through, coordinating teams, and ensuring those big ideas became real. But from the outside, few people understood my role. To some, I looked like a quiet helper in the background.

In one of those roles, I oversaw the day-to-day operations and was very much involved in the strategic direction. Yet, when I applied to be the Executive Director of a sister nonprofit, I realized people didn't see me as a leader. They didn't even know what I had done. And honestly? That was on me.

I had not documented or shared my contributions. I had let others take credit. I assumed people were paying attention. But they weren't. They were busy, distracted, focused on their own responsibilities.

That experience was eye-opening—and painful. From that moment on, I promised myself: I would learn to brag. But I would do it strategically.

## Bragging Isn't Boasting—It's Visibility

The word 'brag' makes many of us uncomfortable. It feels self-serving. But we need to reframe what it means.

Bragging—done well—is not about arrogance. It's about visibility.

It's about making sure your work is seen, valued, and credited.

It's about making sure you are not overlooked when opportunity comes knocking.

We all know someone who takes credit for work they didn't do. That's not bragging, that's theft. What I'm talking about is making sure your genuine contributions are visible—to your supervisors, your colleagues, and your professional network.

## Social Media Can Be a Tool

One of the most helpful tools I've embraced is LinkedIn. I use it to share my professional milestones, amplify the success of others, and document my own leadership story. Social media can feel performative, but if used with authenticity, it becomes a professional archive and personal brand builder.

When you lead a project, speak at a conference, mentor someone, or publish an article—share it. Not just for likes, but for legacy.

This kind of digital visibility:
- Keeps your network aware of your work.
- Demonstrates credibility to future employers.
- Makes it easier to advocate for yourself during reviews or job searches.

## Bragging at Work: Document and Share

Bragging shouldn't only happen online. It should be part of your workplace routine.

Most people assume their boss knows everything they do. That's rarely true.

Here's what I recommend:
- Keep a running list of your wins throughout the year.
- Send a quarterly accomplishments email to your supervisor.
- Prepare a clear, concise end-of-year summary that highlights your impact.

Make it easy for your leaders to advocate for you. Don't make them guess. And don't wait until your annual review to scramble for receipts.

## The Marketing Statement

One of the best pieces of advice I ever received was this: *write a marketing statement.* No more than 20 words.

A marketing statement is a concise summary of what you bring to the table. It forces clarity and intention about your skills, values, and expertise.

Here's mine:

*Experienced nonprofit leader and advocate. Strategic communicator mobilizing people into action. Deep knowledge of Latino communities and public engagement.*

That's 20 words. And every word counts.

Your marketing statement can serve as:
- Your LinkedIn headline.
- Your resume summary.
- The opening line in an interview.
- The closing line when someone asks, *"So, what do you do?"*

Take the time to write yours. Then practice it. Refine it as your career evolves.


## Elevator Pitch: Be Memorable

Once you have your marketing statement, expand it into a short, memorable elevator pitch—a 30-second introduction that sparks curiosity.

It should communicate:
- Who you are.
- What you do (or what you're studying/working toward).
- What makes you unique.

It's called an elevator pitch because you should be able to share it in the time it takes to ride a few floors with someone. It's not your life story. It's your highlight reel.

Here's the truth: most people want to be helpful—especially to students and early-career professionals. But they can't help you if they don't understand who you are and what you're aiming for.

So the next time you're at a networking event, a conference, or even a family gathering, and someone asks, "What do you do?"—be ready.

## Don't Forget the Follow-Up

Meeting someone is just the beginning. What matters just as much is what happens after.

Send a quick email or LinkedIn message:
- Thank them for their time.
- Mention something specific from your conversation.
- Share a resource or ask for a follow-up chat.

Make your follow-up memorable and authentic. People will remember your effort—and it opens the door to stay in touch, ask for advice, or share your resume in the future.

When you make it easy for others to help you, many will.

## Final Thoughts

Learning to brag isn't about ego. It's about owning your power.

It's about understanding that your story, your skills, and your struggles all matter—and that they're worth sharing.

You deserve to be seen. You deserve to be recognized. And if no one else is going to do it for you, you owe it to yourself to do it strategically, gracefully, and consistently.

So go ahead—learn to brag. The right people won't be turned off. They'll be cheering you on.

Learning to brag is about making sure your work is visible. But visibility alone isn't enough. To grow, you also need to let others show up for you. That means unlearning one of the hardest myths many of us carry: that asking for help is weakness.

## REFLECTION & PRACTICE: OWN YOUR BRILLIANCE – BRAG STRATEGICALLY

Use this reflection space as your personal journal to reflect on your accomplishments and practice sharing them. Bragging – when done strategically and authentically – helps others see your impact.

## Step 1: Write Your 20-Word Marketing Statement

*In 20 words or fewer, describe what you bring to the table. Focus on your strengths, values, and unique expertise.* Example: Experienced nonprofit leader and advocate. Strategic communicator mobilizing people into action. Deep knowledge of Latino communities and public engagement.

## Step 2: Draft Your Elevator Pitch

*Create a 30-second introduction that includes: Who you are, what you do (or what you're working toward), what makes you unique.* Write it here in 3–5 sentences. This is your highlight reel, not your life story.

## Step 3: Track and Share Your Wins

List recent accomplishments or projects you've worked on. Be specific about your contributions and their impact (key contribution, outcome or impact). Think of this as your personal *brag notes*— helpful to review for performance reviews, resumes, or LinkedIn posts.

# KEY TAKEAWAYS

Visibility is not arrogance — it's making your work and impact known so opportunities can find you.

Bragging can be reframed as sharing: highlight growth, contributions, and lessons learned in authentic ways.

The more you practice telling your story, the easier it becomes to speak about your achievements with confidence.

# Notes & Reflections

Use this space to capture your thoughts, insights, or next steps

_____

_____

_____

_____

_____

_____

_____

_____

_____

_____

_____

_____

_____

_____

_____

_____

_____

_____

_____

Every reflection adds another layer beneath your iceberg.

Chapter 7

# ASKING FOR HELP IS A STRENGTH, NOT A WEAKNESS

For a long time, I believed I had to do everything on my own.

I was *la mujer fuerte*—the strong woman. Independent. Driven. Unstoppable.

The one who showed up early, stayed late, handled it all without complaint.

The one others could always count on.

I wore that identity like a badge of honor.

But over time, that badge began to feel less like honor and more like armor. Heavy and exhausting.

So many of us grow up internalizing the belief that asking for help is a sign of weakness. That we should be able to figure it out on our own. Push through. Keep it together. We don't want to burden others. We tell ourselves that everyone else already has too much going on. We think: I should be able to do this. I'll be fine. I don't want to seem incapable.

As women of color, as daughters of immigrants, as first-generation professionals—we carry an added weight. The pressure to prove ourselves. To make our families proud. To not mess it up. And somewhere along the way, we equate asking for help with failure.

But here's the truth: even the strongest among us need help. And asking for help is not a weakness.

It's wisdom.
It's strength.
It's trust.

When you ask for help, you give someone else the opportunity to show up for you. You open the door to connection. You create space for reciprocity, for healing, for community. That act of vulnerability can deepen relationships. It reminds us that we don't have to walk this journey alone.

We are not meant to be lone warriors.
We are meant to walk *juntas*. Together.

Let's stop glorifying isolation and start celebrating interdependence. Let's kill the myth of the self-made person. No one does it alone—not really.

As the old proverb says: *If you want to go fast, go alone. If you want to go far, go together.*

## Cultural Narratives and Barriers

Many of us grew up with powerful role models who did everything themselves—our parents, *abuelos, tías*. Many were immigrants who came to another country with very little and few connections. We saw them make sacrifices and hold entire families together. But rarely did we see them ask for help, not because they didn't need it, but because they didn't feel they had the option.

And so, we inherited the same mindset.
We admired their resilience. We learned to be self-reliant.
But in the process, we also learned to carry too much. To silence our needs. To confuse independence with isolation.

It's time to reframe what strength looks like.

Asking for help is not defeat—it's courage.
It doesn't mean you're incapable. It means you're resourceful.
It means you trust yourself enough to know that support will only make you stronger.

## Practical Ways to Ask for Help

If asking for help feels unfamiliar or uncomfortable, here are some ways to begin:

- **Be clear and specific:** Instead of saying "I need help," try "Could you review my resume this week?" or "Would you be open to a 15-minute call to share how you got into your field?"
- **Start with someone you trust:** Ask a mentor, a colleague, or a friend—someone who knows you and wants to see you succeed.
- **Offer reciprocity:** Relationships grow stronger when there's mutual support. A simple "Let me know how I can support you, too" goes a long way.
- **Release the guilt:** Most people *want* to help. Helping others gives us purpose and connection. You're not a burden—you're an opportunity for someone else to be generous.
- **Practice:** Like any skill, it gets easier the more you do it. Start small and build from there.

## An Invitation

You don't have to do it all.
You don't have to know it all.
You just have to be open to asking.
There is power in community.
There is growth in collaboration.
There is healing in being seen and supported.

So let's make it a practice. Let's normalize asking. Let's invite connection. Let's grow—together.

Independence will get you started, but community will take you farther.

In the next section, we'll turn to how your own story—rooted in struggle, resilience, and growth—can become a source of strength for you and inspiration for others.

Relationships, reciprocity, and asking for help expand your support system—but support is only part of the picture. True freedom comes when you combine social capital with financial flexibility and a sense of purpose. In Part III, we'll shift from building connections to exploring possibility: how to create choices for yourself, design your next chapter, and align your life with what matters most.

## REFLECTION & PRACTICE: ASKING FOR HELP

This chapter is about reframing strength. Take a few minutes to reflect on your own relationship with asking for help. Write your answers directly in this book. Be honest with yourself — these reflections are for you, and they may reveal patterns you haven't noticed before.

When was the last time you asked for help? What was the outcome?

What beliefs do you hold about independence, strength, and self-reliance?

Is there something in your life or work right now that would feel lighter with support?

## Practice: Drafting a Request for Help

Asking for help can feel uncomfortable at first, so let's practice in a low-stakes way.

### Step 1. Choose a Need

Think of one area in your life or work where support would make a difference. *(Example: resume feedback, career advice, proofreading a document.)*

### Step 2. Write Your Request

Draft a short message you could send. Keep it clear and specific.

> "Hi [Name], I admire the work you've done in [field]. Would you be open to a 15-minute call next week so I can learn about your career path?"
>
> or
>
> "Hi [Name], I'm applying for a new role and would value your perspective. Would you be open to taking a quick look at my resume and sharing any feedback?"

### Step 3: Pay It Forward

You may not have something to offer in return right now, but you can show that you value reciprocity by helping others when you can.

> "I appreciate your time and advice. I look forward to paying it forward when someone asks me for guidance."

Write it down now — even if you don't send it yet. Practicing the language makes it easier when the moment comes.

# KEY TAKEAWAYS

Success may look individual on the surface, but support, advice, and connections often play a key role.

Asking and giving are connected; reciprocity makes support systems sustainable.

Seeking help is not a weakness it's a strategy that expands your resources, perspective, and possibilities.

# Notes & Reflections

Use this space to capture your thoughts, insights, or next steps

_____
_____
_____
_____
_____
_____
_____
_____
_____
_____
_____
_____
_____
_____
_____
_____
_____
_____
_____

Every reflection adds another layer beneath your iceberg.

# PART THREE

## YOUR STORY, YOUR FUTURE—
### *LIVE WITH INTENTION*

*There is more to life than increasing its speed.*
*Mahatma Gandhi*

*So far, you've explored visibility, confidence, and community —the outer layers of success. Now it's time to turn inward and connect those lessons to your own journey. Part III is about integration: recognizing how your story, experiences, and choices have shaped who you are and where you're headed. Here, you'll look back to understand your growth, and look forward to imagine your future. This is where everything comes together—the self-awareness, the courage, and the connections —to help you design a life guided by purpose and meaning.*

# Chapter 8

# WHAT'S NEXT?

The most important lesson my career taught me is this: you don't need to know what you want to do for the rest of your life.

In fact, you might never have a single answer to that question—and that's okay.

Some people have always known what they wanted to do—and they actually get to do it. That was never me. I didn't have a five-year plan. I admired those who did, but I had to learn how to trust a different process. I went with the flow—but not without intention. I worked hard, I protected my brand, I stayed open, and I networked relentlessly. And when it was time to move on from a good job, I listened to that inner voice and made the leap. Again and again.

Some of the best opportunities I've had came through people I met—friends, colleagues, mentors, even acquaintances who saw my value and made a connection. Networking wasn't just a strategy. It was a lifeline. Without it, I wouldn't have heard about half the jobs that shaped my career.

And then there are some of us—maybe more than we admit—who are still wondering at 40 what we want to do for the rest of our lives. That question used to bother me. The not-knowing felt uneasy. But I've since learned to embrace the question mark. Because that question—*"What's next?"*—is the right question.

Changing jobs, switching sectors, and exploring different career paths worked out beautifully for me, even if it didn't always feel that way in the moment. Now I can look back and see how every twist and turn led me exactly where I was meant to go. But when I was younger, the pressure to have it all figured out felt heavy.

Every turn in my career added a layer beneath my iceberg—skills, lessons, and resilience that weren't obvious at the time but gave me the foundation to take the next leap.

Here's the truth:
- I didn't know what I wanted to be at 20.
- I hadn't figured it all out by 30.
- And even at 40, I was still uncovering new passions and possibilities.

When I share this with college students or early-career professionals, I often see visible relief. There's a false expectation—one that so many of us carry—that we should have a clear, linear plan. But life rarely works that way. Our paths are shaped by curiosity, unexpected opportunities, and the people we meet along the way.

I studied computer science because my dad suggested it. And while I'm grateful for his guidance, I quickly realized that wasn't my calling. I didn't love it. It didn't spark my joy. That realization, as unsettling as it was, pushed me to explore other paths.

Over the course of my career, I've worked for nine different employers. Each job gave me something: a skill, a connection, a lesson. And those experiences—layered over time—helped me find my purpose. It didn't come all at once. It was a journey of asking questions, listening to my gut, and having the courage to make bold moves—even when the next step was unclear.

Some of my biggest leaps came with uncertainty. Leaving a stable job to pursue something unknown. Moving across the country. Starting over. My faith often gave me the courage to take those steps, even when they didn't make sense on paper. Looking back, those moves were the right ones — because while financial security is important, life is also about purpose, growth, and fulfillment.

## The Lesson of the Freedom Fund

When I was moving from Arlington, Virginia back to California, I hit a wall. I had underestimated the cost of the move—packing, shipping, deposits—and before I knew it, my bank account was drained. I remember sitting there, frustrated and embarrassed.

Then, to my huge surprise, I found an uncashed check from my employer. That check saved me. But I was still angry at myself for being in that situation.

That moment taught me something I wish I had understood earlier: transitions are a lot less stressful when you have savings that give you options. At the time, I didn't have what my friend Lisa later called a *Freedom Fund*.

An emergency fund is about survival—car repairs, medical bills, unexpected crises. A Freedom Fund is about *choice*. It's the savings that let you:
- Walk away from a toxic job without fear.
- Take time off to care for yourself or a loved one.
- Go back to school or invest in training.

- Launch a business or passion project.
- Say yes to an opportunity—or no to something that drains you.

I didn't always have that flexibility, and I felt the weight of it in moments like that cross-country move. I want you to have more options. Over time, your Freedom Fund becomes the cushion that gives you confidence to answer the question *"What's next?"* from a place of strength instead of scarcity.

## Building Your Freedom Fund

Here's the truth: saving can feel impossible when you're just getting by. But it's not about big amounts—it's about consistency. Even $10, set aside regularly, builds momentum.

Tips to start:
- Open a separate savings account just for your Freedom Fund.
- Automate a small transfer each paycheck.
- Treat it like a bill to your future self—non-negotiable.
- Keep going. Momentum matters more than perfection.

Remember: social capital and financial capital work together. Mentors, sponsors, and networks open doors — but your Freedom Fund gives you the freedom to walk through them on your own terms.

I'm certainly not a financial advisor, and I could have done much better. But that's exactly why I'm sharing this here — to encourage you to start saving and work toward your own financial freedom. The importance of credit is something many of us don't learn at home or in school, yet it matters deeply. Appendix B includes practical steps for reviewing your credit report.

## Life Is Made of Chapters

Not everyone's journey will look like mine—and that's the point. We each have our own definition of success, our own timeline, and our own seasons of growth.

The real question isn't "What do I want to do forever?"

The better, more powerful question is: "What's next?"

Life doesn't unfold in a straight line. It moves in chapters—some short, some long, some joyful, others challenging. Each chapter brings new opportunities to evolve. You may be in a season of transition, a season of waiting, or a season of reinvention. All of them are valid.

You don't have to know the entire path to take the next step. And sometimes, that next step is enough.

## The Myth of Having It All Figured Out

We live in a culture that glorifies certainty and long-term plans. But some of the most incredible opportunities I've had came from saying yes to something small, something I wasn't sure about, something that felt a little scary:

- Leaving a job.
- Moving cities.
- Applying for a program.
- Asking a new contact to meet for coffee.

That's how you uncover what's next—not by having all the answers, but by being willing to explore.

## Coaching Helps

When I was in transition—uncertain about what was next for me professionally—I worked with a coach. During our six months together, I didn't receive answers handed to me. Instead, through reflective questions and deep listening, she helped me uncover the answers that were already within me.

I discovered I was searching for three things:

- **Purpose:** I wanted to continue making a difference.
- **Visibility:** I wanted to step forward as a Latina leader, to be a role model others could see.
- **Autonomy:** I wanted the freedom to shape a vision, not just execute someone else's.

That clarity helped me stay grounded. It prevented me from jumping at the first opportunity and gave me the courage to say no when roles didn't align. That coaching experience was so transformative that I eventually became a coach myself.

## Design Your Next Chapter

I often ask coaching clients:
- What excites you right now?
- What are you curious about?
- What are you tired of?
- What are you craving more of?

These are clues. Don't ignore them.

*Ask yourself: What's one thing I could do in the next 30 days that would move me forward, even just a little?*

It might be updating your resume.
Having a conversation with someone in a role you admire.
Signing up for a workshop.

Small steps count. And they often lead to bigger doors.

And here's the freedom that comes with taking those small steps: you're not locked into one version of your life. You always have permission to reimagine who you are and what you do.

## You Get to Reimagine
You don't have to stick to one career or one identity.

You are allowed to change. To grow. To pivot.
- You can go back to school at 50.
- Start a business after retirement.
- Take a sabbatical.
- Try something new, even if it makes no sense to anyone else.

You don't need permission to evolve. You just need courage—and a little clarity.

This chapter is your invitation to explore. To imagine. To begin again.

You are not too late.
You are not behind.
You are exactly where you need to be.

So, what's next?

## Closing Thoughts

Remember, *"What's next?"* isn't about pressure—it's about possibility. You don't need a 30-year plan. You just need the courage to take one step forward, to trust that clarity comes with movement, and to stay open to the people and opportunities that appear along the way.

Every season, every chapter, adds to the story of who you are becoming. And the beautiful truth is this: you are never behind, and it is never too late. Your next chapter is waiting—and you get to write it.

And as you begin to explore what's next, the question naturally deepens: *What is my purpose?* In the next chapter, we'll walk through how to uncover and define yours—so your next step isn't just forward, but aligned.

## REFLECTION & PRACTICE: WHAT'S NEXT FOR YOU?

Reflect on your next chapter—whether you're stepping into a new role, considering a change, or simply feeling uncertain. Process your thoughts and begin building momentum, one step at a time.

## Step 1: Reflecting on the Present

What parts of your life or work feel aligned and fulfilling right now?
What parts feel out of alignment or draining your energy?

What are you most curious about these days? What's pulling at your attention?

If you could hit pause and do anything for the next year, what would it be — and why?

## Step 2: Looking at Your Past for Clues

Think about the last time you felt proud of yourself. What were you doing, and what did it take to get there?

What activities or moments make you feel energized and engaged?

Have there been times when a small step led to a big opportunity? What were they?

## Designing What's Next

*If you could ask one bold question about your future, what would it be?*

*What fears or limiting beliefs are holding you back from exploring what's next?*

*What support or resources would make the next step easier for you?*

What is one action you can take this week to move closer to your next chapter?

Who can you share this goal with to help keep you accountable?

## KEY TAKEAWAYS

Careers are rarely linear — you don't need a 30-year plan, just the courage to take the next step.

Social capital opens doors, and financial cushions like a Freedom Fund give you the flexibility to walk through them on your own terms.

You always have permission to evolve. Life moves in chapters, and you get to design the next one.

# Notes & Reflections

*Use this space to capture your thoughts, insights, or next steps*

_____

_____

_____

_____

_____

_____

_____

_____

_____

_____

_____

_____

_____

_____

_____

_____

_____

_____

_____

*Every reflection adds another layer beneath your iceberg.*

Chapter 9

# FINDING YOUR PURPOSE

In the last chapter, we explored the question *"What's next?"*—a question that opens doors and helps you take the next step forward. But "what's next?" only becomes truly powerful when it's connected to something deeper: your purpose.

I believe life is about finding your purpose.

The big questions — *Who am I? Why am I here?* — have echoed in my mind for as long as I can remember. I found journals I wrote as a teenager wondering what my purpose was. I didn't know it then, but I was asking the same questions philosophers, spiritual leaders, and seekers have asked across time. I was searching for my purpose.

As I grew older, I realized these questions don't have easy or permanent answers. But that doesn't mean they don't matter. In fact, I've come to believe that *our purpose isn't just something we find — it's something we live into.*

## Purpose as Identity

Philosopher Josiah Royce[7] said that the question *"Who am I?"* cannot be

---

[7] Philosopher Josiah Royce explored the idea of purpose and identity in works such as *The Philosophy of Loyalty* (1908). By "loyalty," he didn't just mean being faithful to a person or group. He meant a deep commitment to a cause or ideal beyond ourselves — a devotion that gives life meaning and helps define who we are.

answered without reference to purpose. Our name, our background, our origin stories — they may describe us, but they don't define us. Royce believed that true identity is found not in labels, but in our loyalty to a cause or ideal — something greater than ourselves.

Our purpose is not handed to us at birth; it's revealed over time — like a puzzle, with each piece earned through experience. Some people find it early, some late, and some may spend their entire lives searching. But that search itself — that hunger for meaning — matters.

When we are loyal to a purpose, when we live for something greater than ourselves, we begin to answer the question of who we are. The search for one's true self is, at its core, the search for purpose.

## Purpose as Service

Psychologist Abraham Maslow introduced the well-known *Hierarchy of Needs*,[8] a theory that begins with basic survival — food, shelter, safety — and builds toward self-actualization, the fullest expression of who we can be. I have realized that we don't get to the top of the Maslow pyramid until we focus on using our talents in service of others.

**Maslow's Hierarchy of Needs**

---

[8] Psychologist Abraham Maslow introduced his *Hierarchy of Needs* in a 1943 paper, later expanded in his book *Motivation and Personality* (1954). The theory suggests that human needs build in levels, from basics like food and safety to higher goals like belonging, esteem, and ultimately self-actualization. Maslow's Pyramid first appeared in Charles McDermid's article,"How Money Motivates Men," published in Business Horizons in 1960.

Later thinkers, like Viktor Frankl[9], deepened this truth. Frankl, a Holocaust survivor and psychiatrist, argued that true fulfillment doesn't come from seeking happiness or even self-actualization directly. It comes from forgetting ourselves in service to a greater cause.

In other words, we become who we are meant to be not by focusing on ourselves — but by contributing to others, by lifting up our communities, by answering the call to do good in the world.

## Not Everyone Gets There — But Everyone Can Try

The sobering truth is that not everyone finds their purpose — not because they don't have one, but because life's demands and distractions can drown it out. Many are so busy surviving that they never get the space to ask deeper questions. Others are told that their purpose must look a certain way — tied to money, prestige, or success.

But purpose isn't a job title. It's not a GPA, a paycheck, or a diploma.

Purpose is your unique contribution to the world, shaped by your gifts, your values, and your experiences.

For some, it's raising a family. Your purpose may change throughout your life — but your loyalty to becoming your best self in service of something greater can guide you always.

---

[9] Psychiatrist Viktor Frankl, a Holocaust survivor, shared this insight in his classic book *Man's Search for Meaning* (1946; English translation 1959). He argued that lasting fulfillment is not found by pursuing happiness directly, but by devoting ourselves to a purpose beyond the self.

## A Personal Note

In my own life, I've felt most alive — most aligned — when I've used my voice, my network, and my knowledge to help others rise. That is my purpose. I didn't find it all at once, and it wasn't always clear. But every time I followed curiosity, helped someone, or made a brave choice, I moved one step closer.

This book itself is part of that purpose.

If you're still asking those big questions — good. That means you're still becoming. Keep asking. Keep growing. Keep giving.

Life isn't about having all the answers. It's about staying loyal to the search for meaning — and to the purpose only you can fulfill.

Your iceberg is uniquely yours. The world may see your title, your achievements, or your polished moments, but the real strength comes from what lies beneath: your struggles, your values, your purpose. That unseen foundation is what makes everything above possible.

## Closing Reflection

Purpose isn't a single destination — it's a compass that helps you navigate each season of your life. You don't need it all figured out to live with purpose; you just need to align your next step with what matters most.

As you grow, your purpose may evolve, and that's not a sign of failure—it's a sign of life. Hold your purpose close, let it guide your decisions, and trust that with every choice, you are shaping a life of meaning.

And remember this: your story is still being written. The setbacks, the leaps, the doubts, and the victories—they're all part of your iceberg, the unseen foundation beneath every visible success.

So as you step into your next chapter, keep asking the question that has guided me time and again: *What's next?* And let your purpose be the compass that helps you answer it, one intentional step at a time.

You are not behind. You are not too late. You are exactly where you need to be—and the world is waiting for the contribution only you can make.

## REFLECTION & PRACTICE: TRACING THE CLUES TO YOUR PURPOSE

You don't have to know your purpose today. But you can begin listening for it. Purpose often leaves a trail — in the things that move you, energize you, or won't let you go.

Take 10-15 minutes to journal your responses. Don't edit yourself — just write from the heart.

Then look over what you've written and ask.

*What activities make you feel most alive? When do you lose track of time? What are you doing when you feel the most like yourself?*

*What have people always come to you for? Advice? Encouragement? Creativity? Organizing chaos? What strengths do others see in you, even when you don't see them in yourself?*

What breaks your heart or fires you up? Is there a cause, injustice, or community that stirs something deep in you?

What challenge have you overcome and who else might need your help overcoming it? Sometimes our greatest pain points us toward our greatest purpose.

*What kind of legacy do you want to leave behind? When people talk about your impact someday, what do you hope they'll say?*

*What themes keep showing up? What patterns do you notice?*

## A Note of Gratitude

Thank you for spending this time with me. Writing this book has been both a reflection on my own journey and an offering to yours. My hope is that in these pages you've found not just stories and strategies, but reminders of your own strength, your own resilience, and your own power to create change.

If something here resonated with you, carry it forward. Share it with someone who needs encouragement. Use it to take a brave step of your own. That's how social capital grows—when we lift as we climb, when we open doors for one another, and when we believe that our stories matter.

I am grateful you've allowed me to be part of your story, even in this small way. And I can't wait to see the legacy you build—one connection, one choice, one chapter at a time.

And remember: like an iceberg, the world may only see a fraction of who you are. But beneath the surface lies the depth, wisdom, and purpose that make you unstoppable. Trust in that unseen strength—it's what will carry you forward.

With gratitude and hope,
Dra. Inez

## Acknowledgments

I'd like to thank my sister, Norma González-Jasso, who has encouraged me to follow my dream of becoming an author. My gratitude also goes to my mentor Erica Alfaro, who has made it her mission to guide Latines in turning their stories into books. I always say everyone has a book to write, but figuring out how to make it happen is another story. Through Erica's mentorship, I became part of a community of authors in *Grupo de Escritores*. I know that having a supportive community makes all the difference. Muchas gracias por su apoyo.

## Stay Connected

This book is just the beginning of the conversation. If something here sparked reflection, courage, or curiosity in you, I'd love to stay connected.

**Follow my journey** on [Instagram @coach_inezgp] for reflections, resources, and encouragement.

**Explore coaching with me** if you're ready for deeper support in designing your next chapter. Coaching creates space for clarity, accountability, and growth.

You don't have to walk this path alone. Together, we can continue building the connections, opportunities, and purpose that make life meaningful.

Your story matters. And I'd be honored to be part of your next chapter.

# APPENDIX

## Appendices Overview

These appendices provide additional tools and resources connected to key chapters. They're here if you'd like to go deeper or need practical, step-by-step guidance.

### Appendix A: Is Higher Education Worth It?

(Expands on Chapter 5 and explores data and perspectives on the value of higher education)

Lately, I've heard more people say college isn't worth it. This narrative is growing in media, podcasts, and politics. To me, it feels intentional — aimed at discouraging higher education, especially among working-class and marginalized communities.

And I have to ask: who's saying this? Did these same critics attend college themselves? Did their children? Often, the answer is yes. That's what makes this so troubling. The very people who benefited from college now cast doubt on its value for others.

Let me be clear: college is worth it. Especially when you look at the data.

Below is a table from the U.S. Bureau of Labor Statistics, Current Population Survey[10], which shows the relationship between educational attainment and median weekly earnings.

---

[10] Data from the U.S. Bureau of Labor Statistics, *Current Population Survey, 2024 Annual Averages*. The survey provides monthly and annual information on employment, unemployment, earnings, and other key labor market trends in the United States. https://www.bls.gov/emp/images/ep_chart_001.png

**Earnings and unemployment rates by educational attainment, 2024**

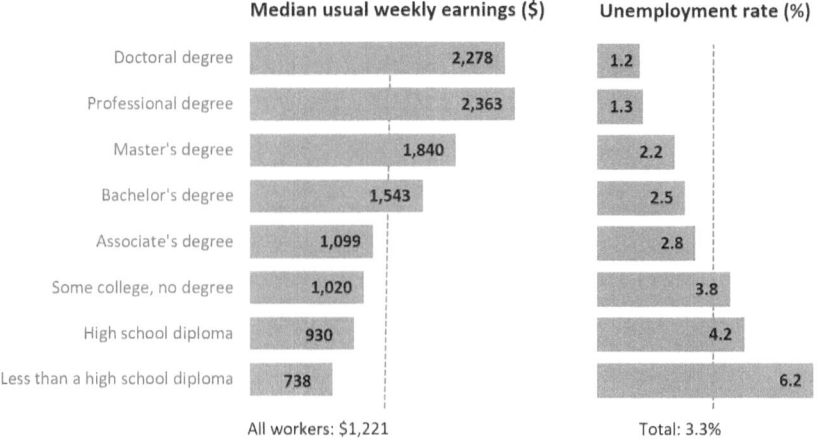

Note: Data are for persons age 25 and over. Earnings are for full-time wage and salary workers.
Source: U.S. Bureau of Labor Statistics, Current Population Survey.

Note: Data are for persons age 25 and over. Earnings are for full-time wage and salary workers.
Source: https://www.bls.gov/emp/images/ep_chart_001.png

The earnings gap between high school graduates and college graduates adds up to hundreds of thousands of dollars over a lifetime. That's real opportunity.

But data isn't the whole story. Not all graduates experience the same return. Some struggle to find jobs in their field. Others graduate burdened with debt. The missing piece is often social capital — knowing how to navigate the system, build relationships, and access opportunities.

This is true in the workplace too. Degrees and titles help, but long-term success depends on how you keep learning, growing, and building connections.

Of course, not everyone needs a degree. Certificate programs, apprenticeships, coding bootcamps, and skilled trades can also lead to rewarding careers. But even with alternatives, higher education remains one of the most powerful tools for mobility, discovery, and long-term success.

So, is college worth it? Yes — especially if you approach it with intention, build relationships along the way, and take advantage of opportunities.

**Appendix B: Understanding Your Credit Report**

(Expands on Chapter 8 and offers a practical guide to reviewing your credit, building financial literacy, and planning ahead.)

Your Freedom Fund is about choice and agency. To build it wisely, you need to know where you stand financially — and that means knowing your credit. Credit isn't just about borrowing money. It affects whether you can rent an apartment, qualify for a loan, or even get certain jobs. Think of it as part of your social capital with financial institutions: it tells others whether you're reliable and trustworthy.

Your credit score doesn't just affect credit cards—it can impact renting an apartment, car loans, and interest rates.

I had delinquent accounts in my twenties and thirties. Eventually I faced them: I paid them off one by one, closed the cards that weren't helping me, and rebuilt. It wasn't easy, but it was possible. Today my credit score is strong because I stayed consistent.

**Quick refresher**
**Credit report** = a list of your accounts and payment history.

Credit score = a number based on that report. For FICO Scores the biggest factors are payment history and amounts owed/"utilization."

**Step 1. How to Access Your Free Credit Report**
You're entitled to one free credit report every year from each of the three major credit bureaus (Equifax, Experian, and TransUnion).

**Where to go:** AnnualCreditReport.com (the only official site). You now get free weekly online credit reports from Equifax, Experian and TransUnion - no credit card required.

**What you'll need:** your Social Security number, current and past addresses, and answers to identity questions, (they may ask about past loans or addresses).

**How to do it (5–10 minutes):**
1. Go to **AnnualCreditReport.com** and click **Request your free credit reports.**
2. Choose which bureau you want first (Equifax, Experian, or TransUnion). You can do all three at once or spread them out.
3. Answer the identity questions and download/save the PDF of your report to a secure folder.
4. If online verification doesn't work, follow the instructions to request by phone or mail.

Tip: Some people check one bureau each month (Equifax in January, Experian in February, TransUnion in March, and repeat). That way, you're keeping an eye on your credit year-round without feeling overwhelmed.

Safety note: If a site asks for a credit card or subscription, you're in the wrong place. Stick with AnnualCreditReport.com — it's the official one.

**Step 2 — What to Look For**
As you review your report:
- Personal information: Make sure your name, address, and social security number are correct.
- Accounts: Check that your credit cards, loans, and payment history are accurate.

- Errors or fraud: Look for accounts you don't recognize, incorrect balances, or missed payments you know you made.
- Inquiries: Review who has checked your credit.

If you find mistakes, dispute them directly with the credit bureau.

**Don't panic if you see something scary.** Many people who pull a report for the first time see late payments, collections, or balances that feel overwhelming. The key is not to ignore them—this guide gives you steps to fix them.

### Step 3 — Fix what's wrong (disputes)
If you find errors, dispute them with the bureau that shows the mistake (Equifax, Experian, or TransUnion). You can do this online from each bureau's site.

**What to include:**
- A short statement of what's wrong ("This account is not mine," "Balance is incorrect," etc.)
- Proof (statements, letters, police report if identity theft)
- Your ID (as requested by the bureau)

They typically have 30 days to investigate and respond. Keep copies of everything.

**Quick template (paste into the bureau's dispute form):**

"I am disputing [account name/number]. The [issue] is inaccurate. Please investigate and correct or delete this item. I've attached [documents] supporting my claim."

### Step 4 — If the debt is yours (triage & scripts)
**Prioritize** (top to bottom):
1. Bring all open accounts current (avoid new late marks).

2. Tackle small balances you can clear quickly (wins help momentum).
3. Negotiate collections/charged-off debts—aim to settle in writing.

**Call script for a collector (write down name/date):**
"I'd like to resolve account [number]. The balance shows $____. I can pay $____ by [date] if you agree in writing that the account will be reported as paid (or settled) and the balance updated to $0. Please send the letter or email, and I'll pay as soon as I receive it."

Some collectors will agree to update how they report an account after payment; get **everything in** writing before you pay. (Be cautious with "pay-for-delete"—policies vary.)

Important to know: Paying a legitimate collection won't restart the reporting clock. Most negative marks (like late payments, collections, or charge-offs) drop off your credit report **after seven years from the first missed payment.** That means the sooner you face it, the sooner the countdown begins. One day, that negative mark will disappear—and your credit will reflect your progress.

### Step 5 — Build (or rebuild) positive history
These moves build points over time:
- Autopay the minimum on every open account so you're never late.
- Keep utilization low: try to use under 30% of your limit (under 10% is excellent).
- Leave your oldest card open (if no annual fee).
- Starter options if you're new to credit: a secured card, a small credit-builder loan, or becoming an authorized useron a trusted person's long-standing, on-time account.
- Space out applications to limit hard inquiries (they generally fall off after 2 years).

**Step 6 — Protect your progress (free & fast)**
- Set alerts inside your bank/credit card apps for due dates and large transactions.
- Freeze your credit with each bureau (free) to block new accounts in your name; lift the freeze temporarily when you need to apply. A fraud alert is a lighter option that tells lenders to verify your identity first.

**Step 7 — Rinse & repeat (simple maintenance)**
- Pull one report each month (rotate bureaus) and scan for changes. Free weekly reports make this easy.
- Celebrate small wins (a paid collection, a lower balance, three months on-time).

**Real talk**
I had a few delinquent accounts in my twenties and thirties. One by one, I paid those off, closed the ones that weren't serving me, and fixed my credit score.

Remember: your score is not your worth. It's a tool—and tools can be sharpened.

Financial health is part of the iceberg too. People may notice the car you drive or the home you live in, but what really keeps those things afloat are the unseen layers of discipline, sacrifice, and steady effort beneath the surface.

**Start today**
- Pull your reports.
- Fix any errors.
- Make this month the first of many on-time payments.

It may take years for some marks to fall off, but they *will*. That's why facing them now matters.

Used wisely, cards help you build history. Used carelessly, they get expensive fast.

- Only charge what you can pay off each month.
- Pay on time, every time (autopay the minimum; pay the rest manually).
- Avoid "minimum payment only" habits— interest turns $40 sweater into a $60 + sweater over months.

**Build your Financial Literacy**

- Take a free or low-cost personal finance class (library, community college, nonprofit).
- Follow educators who speak your language.
- Ask "basic" questions. We learn by asking.

## About the Author

Dr. Inez González Perezchica is a recognized advocate for equity, education, and leadership. She was the founding director of the Latino Communications Institute at Cal State Fullerton, a pioneering workforce-preparedness initiative for first-generation college students pursuing media and communications careers. She spent nearly a decade shaping policy and advocacy at the National Hispanic Media Coalition, where she worked on issues of media representation and civil rights.

A lifelong learner and leadership coach, Dr. González Perezchica has participated in some of the nation's most respected leadership programs, including the HOPE Leadership Institute, the National Hispana Leadership Institute, the Women's Policy Institute, and LEAD San Diego. She holds a B.S. in Computer Science from the University of San Diego, an M.A. in Organizational Management from the University of Phoenix, an M.P.A. from Harvard University's Kennedy School of Government, and an Ed.D. in Educational Leadership from Cal State Fullerton. She is also a Board Certified Coach with a Leadership Coaching Certificate from the University of San Diego's School of Leadership and Education Sciences.

Dr. González Perezchica has been honored widely for her contributions to community, advocacy, and leadership. The Mayor of San Diego proclaimed a "Dr. Inez González Perezchica Day" in her honor. She was named one of the 500 Most Influential People in San Diego by the *San Diego Business Journal,* received the Social Mobility & Advancement Leader of the Year Award from Cause San Diego, and was recognized as a Girl Scouts San Diego Cool Woman.

A proud binational citizen, she was born and raised in Tijuana, México, and continues to bridge cultures, communities, and generations in everything she does.

## About the Publisher

Riot of Roses Publishing House is a radical feminist, award-winning press that was founded in 2021 to amplify the stories of historically silenced voices and narratives.

Xicana owned. Mujerista focused. For the people.

We publish books that heal and liberate.

Read our rebellion.

Find & follow us @riotofrosespublishing
Visit us at www.riotofrosespublishinghouse.com

Riot of Roses Publishing House offers bulk quantity discounts to educational institutions, businesses, and community groups. For more information, reach out to us at riotofrosesllc@gmail.com

**RIOT OF ROSES**
PUBLISHING HOUSE
SEJATNGA
UNCEDED TONGVA TERRITORY
SOUTH WHITTIER, CALIFORNIA

www.ingramcontent.com/pod-product-compliance
Lightning Source LLC
Chambersburg PA
CBHW021150130626
46554CB00005B/1739